Isaac Williams

**The Cathedral**

The Catholic and Apostolic Church in England

Isaac Williams

**The Cathedral**
*The Catholic and Apostolic Church in England*

ISBN/EAN: 9783337405151

Printed in Europe, USA, Canada, Australia, Japan

Cover: Foto ©Lupo / pixelio.de

More available books at **www.hansebooks.com**

OR THE

# CATHOLIC AND APOSTOLIC CHURCH

# IN ENGLAND

BY

# ISAAC WILLIAMS, B. D.

EDITED WITH NOTES AND INTRODUCTION BY REV. W. BENHAM, B.D.; F.S.A.

RECTOR OF ST EDMUND'S, LOMBARD STREET

"The house of God, which is the Church of the living God, the pillar and ground of the truth." – 1 TIM. iii. 15.

LONDON

GRIFFITH, FARRAN, OKEDEN & WELSH

(SUCCESSORS TO NEWBERY AND HARRIS)

AND SYDNEY, N.S.W.

1889

# INTRODUCTORY ANALYSIS OF
## "THE CATHEDRAL."

THE Prefatory Sonnet, "The Approach," indicates at once the central idea of the Pcem. The author, in the calm twilight and stillness of Eventide, meditates upon the beautiful pile, looking, with all its pinnacles and spires, like a grove in deep repose, and through its open door beholds, symbolised by the gloom, the woes which afflict mankind; and yet in the midst there is a vista of light leading to the unfading day. And the key to that blest road is held by the Wisdom which is from above, by the heavenly Wealth which the world esteems poverty. To their key the white door opens, and displays treasures which, spiritually discerned, are found to be not of earth but of Heaven.

And so he approaches the Western Front. It is entered in all great Cathedrals by a triple door, two lowly, the middle lofty; and the poet sees herein the symbol of what is required of those who seek admission into the Church of Christ,—Repentance, Faith, Obedience. His meditation on the first of these, in which he expatiates on the need of a daily Repentance until the end of life shall bring rest and light, is singularly beautiful. That on the main portal, Obedience, is characteristic as expressing one great principle of the Oxford Tract writers, namely, the protest against Religious " Liberalism." Self-denial, Self-restraint, in regard both to bodily comfort and mental liberty, must be practised by those who would explore the glories which God shall reveal to those only who seek Him in humility.

The poem on Faith, though very sweet and beautiful, is somewhat obscure in its opening. The two first lines are adjectival clauses, in apposition with the subject "Faith." "Faith, a wanderer through the vale of years, and her feet being bent towards the west, hath made," &c. The westward pilgrimage, of course, is from the place of the birth of the Dayspring from whom our religion has come. The "last retreat" is the final settlement, because she has traversed the whole earth, and from the ends of it looks forward to return with restored man to Paradise again. She has taken up her abode in the pillared shrine, and it is by her that the rites of the Church become full of living power, means and channels of Divine grace. Having entered, the poet makes his way to the Cloisters, there to meditate upon the general System and Forms of the Church, whom he addresses in the second person as the "Ancient of Mothers," who in her parental love is all the year round offering daily to her children treasures that wax not old (i.). Earthly Love, he says, whether of Home, or Friend, or Kindred, throws a charm over the commonest concerns and features of life; even so does the faithful soul see in every mute form of Mother Church something to cherish and love. And under her holy spell the Forms which hold the soul bound are dearer than un-fettered liberty (ii.). His meditations as he passes along, on Prayer, on Sunday, on Village Churches and Cathedrals, lead him on to the Churches of Scotland and Wales; the latter causing him deep grief because of the prevalence of Dissent, where once had been a saintly British Church : and this again brings him back to meditate with anxiety on the present aspect of political affairs in relation to the Church. It must be remembered that the movements of the Whig party after the passing of the Reform Bill of 1832 were causing great alarm to earnest Churchmen. Lord Grey had told the Bishops to set their house in order; some of the prelates had been insulted ; the Irish Church was fiercely attacked. It was all this, in fact, which first caused Newman to start the Tracts. (*Apologia*, p. 93.) Hence Mr Williams, writing at that anxious time, says :—" We have lost our bearings, and discern nothing of our whereabouts except the tracks of the past" (sonnet xvi.). But his faith is assured that amid all the changes of the world God will protect His own, and he fixes his eyes on the vision of the City of God (xxi.). He returns for a while to warn against the spirit of selfishness and impatience (xxii.), and to pray for the spirit of Self-sacrifice (xxiii.). Next, in five sonnets, he explains the custom of obeisance to the East. There is the Altar which supplies our life (xxiv.), our thoughts are carried, as we gaze eastwards, over lands which have been the homes of great saints of the Church (xxv.), onwards to the land where Jesus lived and died (xxvi.) ; and to our lost Eden (xxvii.) ; and, lastly, we think of the coming of Christ, the final rising of the Sun of Righteousness upon the earth (xxviii.).

He passes on towards *The Chapter House.* Memories of the perfect calm and stillness of nature in given circumstances crowd into his mind, and in the stillness he feels himself alone with God. The blue haze of the summer's day is to him as the tent of the Most High, and out of it He speaks eloquently. The poet in answer pours forth his supplication for light and love. Far away he sees a flock of birds making their way homewards, and it enkindles within him the hope that at length he shall flee away from the world's turmoil, and be at rest.

The thoughts on the *Chapter House* are suggested by a passage from St Ignatius, which he quotes at the beginning of this poem, in which the saint compares the union of the Presbytery with the Bishop to that of the strings of a harp. Though eye cannot see, nor ear hear it, such a harmony there is, heard in heaven. It is the part of the believing soul to listen for the echoes of that harmony, and to bow before it. For while the Sovereignty of God is committed in part to earthly kings, the Priesthood of Christ is exercised directly by Himself in His Ordinances, His garment filled with healing, His people fed from apostolic hands.

Then (iv.) the poet returns to look with sorrow at the world despising His gifts and persecuting His Church. He calls on the Church to behold in the world's hate a note of Christ's favour; the good which it offers is poison to the proud and grief to the humble, whilst they who are persecuted for righteousness' sake are blessed. Not only shall they receive Christ's crown at last, but even now God dwells in them, and their faith sheds light upon all around them.

The poet passes next to the *North Porch*, for he imagines a uniformity in the architecture (see his note at the end). The North Porch suggests, in its bleak outlook, thoughts of the Church in trouble and anxiety, and he proceeds to gather instances where God gave comfort in dark times.

The *Sepulchral Recesses* suggest to him, on the one side, thoughts of martyrs and confessors of the Church of England; on the other, of great benefactors.

Passing into the *Oratories*, or side-chapels, he describes himself as listening to the Choral Service which has resounded through the Cathedral, and is now dying away into silence. He imagines this divine worship passing upwards, even into Heaven, and bearing the praises of the Lamb that was slain. The setting sun reminds him of the Incarnation, the Eternal Son "hath gone down to man." The stanzas in which he sings of this are, as he says in a note, suggested by a striking poem of George Herbert's, of which we will quote three verses.

> " Hast thou not heard that my Lord Jesus died ?
> Then let me tell thee a strange story :
> The God of power, as He did ride
> In His majestic robes of glory,
> ᴉ Resolved to 'light, and so one day
> He did descend, undressing all the way.

" The stars His tire of light and rings obtain'd,
The cloud His bow, the fire His spear,
The sky His azure mantle gain'd.
And when they ask'd what He would wear
He smiled, and said as He did go
He had new clothes a-making here below.

" When He was come, as travellers are wont,
He did repair unto an inn,
Both then and after, many a brunt
He did endure to cancel sin ;
And having given the rest before,
Here He gave up His life to pay our score."

In continuation of this thought the poet dwells on the contrast which earth shall present—the crown of thorns instead of glory, the voice of the Baptist in the wilderness, the crowd of penitents. And he closes with the Vision of the Saviour returning to His glory, bearing His own with Him.

In another of the Oratories he meditates on the " doxology," and adduces a multitude of instances of threefold unity. Then he passes to "the Athanasian Creed," on which he dwells as the restraint on license, the fetters which bind us to God. " Fast Days" is the last of the subjects dealt with in the Oratories.

The *Transepts* become to our author the symbols, respectively, of the Psalms and the Epistle and Gospel, " Jesus Christ in Prophecy," and " Jesus Christ in History." And it is evident that in speaking of the Psalter, he has in view not merely the recital of the daily Psalms, but the use of the metrical version in song.

The school to which Mr Isaac Williams belonged, was for a long time hostile to the use of hymns. It was thought that they were irreverent and over-familiar in expression, and too " subjective," dwelling too exclusively on personal experiences. Bishop Mant preached severely against them as an innovation ; and those churches where the metrical

version of the Psalms was not in use, was at once known
as being of an "Evangelical" character.   It will be seen
that in the opening stanzas, and they are very noble, the
main thought is, that in the Psalter Christ is set forth
sometimes dimly, sometimes clearly; and he draws a beautiful moral from the intermingling of the Psalmist's cries
about his enemies and his warfare (stanzas iv.-vii.)   The
strains in which he brings out the deep comfort and
strength of the Psalms to the sorrowful soul are, per-
haps, the most lovely in the whole volume.   He reviews
the works of other poets, men of rare gifts from God's
Holy Spirit, but who went to other wells of inspiration, and
so fell into error (stanzas xxii., xxiii.)   And with these he
contrasts the sweet Psalmist of Israel (xxiv. to end.)

Coming subsequently to the South Transept, the poet
brings out very beautifully the teaching of the .Church
through the successive sacred seasons, and closes with a
plaintive dirge over the destruction wrought by wild
zealots, while he thankfully acknowledges that even yet
we have far more to be thankful for than to deplore.

Coming to *the Nave*, the poet divides it into three portions,
which he names the North, South, and Middle "Aisles."
This is a curious misnomer.   The word "Aisle" is derived
from Lat. *ala*, a wing; the two aisles lie like folded wings
alongside the body of the Church, and the body itself cannot be called one of its wings.   But it is better to leave the
mistake untouched, and to accept our poet's nomenclature
for the time being.   The central aisle represents to him
Holy Scripture, those of the sides, Prayer and the Creed.
He shows how the Lord's Prayer can be applied specially in
each part of the Daily Service, in Holy Communion, and
in the other Offices of the Church, as well as its power in
private devotion.   He has on this occasion given his own
analysis at the head of the poem.   In the "Middle Aisle,"
beginning with a line from Milton's *Samson*, he reiterates this
line again and again all through this poem.   For he is compar-
ing himself with one who is being led on through life, whilst

he has no choice, and no desire, but to be led by a celestial Guide. And such Divine guidance he finds in the Daily Services of the Church, and in hearing the Scriptures read in it. Very touching are the words (§ iii.) in which he recognises that there are mysterious meanings in Holy Writ which may be made known to those who diligently seek to know God's will. In § v. he begins, as he has done with other portions, to follow the Bible method in order, and starting with the Fall he follows the Bible down to the Revelation, always watching to take to himself the lesson which God would have him learn (see p. 121, "Like that fam'd Trojan," &c.). The poem on the Creed, which he finds symbolized in the *South Aisle*, the author has analysed for himself in the heading which he has prefixed to it.

When he comes to the Choir, the steps suggest to him the supplications of the Litany, rising higher and higher to the Throne of Grace. But even these would be poor and valueless, had we not a sure and unfailing hope that Christ Himself will be with us to present our petitions. This is the point of the stanzas entitled "Despondency," under the head of *Approach to the Choir.* The sense deepens upon him of drawing nigh to the Saviour in His own Ordinances. But here he is met by the *Screen*, and it at once becomes the symbol to him of the "Disciplina Arcani." This expression was used by writers of the Mediæval Church to describe that custom of primitive times by which the most important and mysterious doctrines and rites of Christianity were concealed from the unbaptised, and fully developed only to those who were admitted to Holy Communion. Not only the Holy Eucharist itself, but Ordination, and even the Creed and Lord's Prayer were held in reserve until the catechumens were considered to be fully instructed in the elements of the faith. Our author of "The Cathedral" was also the author of one of the *Tracts for the Times* which kindled a vehement opposition (No. 80), "On Religious Reserve," in which he advocated a like Disciplina Arcani, as a remedy against heresy, which comes through perverting doctrines true in themselves. Gieseler, the German Church historian, contends that the *Disciplina Arcani* ceased with heathenism.

Entering *the Choir*, the series of poems culminates in "the Sacramental Hymn." It consists of twelve portions, each containing three strophes, sung respectively by "Men," "Angels," and "Men and Angels." Mankind raises the voice of praise of God's great heavenly glory, the Angels respond with that of His work on earth below, and the Chorus of both speaks of the union of the two. The rich variety of the thoughts, and the close harmony of strophe and antistrophe, so arranged that all culminates in the blessedness of Holy Communion here, and the Marriage Feast in Heaven,—all these things make up a glorious meditation.

*The Lady Chapel*, of course, brings in a poem on the "Magnificat," in which the song of the Blessed Virgin is applied both to the Catholic Church and to the individual soul laying up Christ's words, and keeping them.

The *Pillars of the Nave* and of *the Choir* become, respectively, texts of the Old Testament "Patriarchs and Prophets," and of New Testament "Apostles ;" and the Side Windows, of "Ancient Fathers of the Church." Notes on all these will be found under each. Notes within square brackets are those of the Editor. The remainder are those of the Author.

W. B.

# ADVERTISEMENT.

THE idea upon which this publication has been composed is, it is hoped, perfectly in accordance with the spirit and principles of the Ancient Church; nor is it entirely new to our own. Hints of the kind may be gained from Herbert's "Temple," where he attaches moral and sacred Lessons to the "Church windows" and "Church floor." And it has been suggested by the Author of "The Excursion," in his Preface to that work, that his Poems might be considered as capable of being arranged as the parts of a Gothic Church, of which the minor pieces might be "likened to the little cells, oratories, and sepulchral recesses." The present design has been to execute such a plan by a selection of subjects, more or less appropriate to the parts which they are made to represent, from the Liturgy, and the Doctrine and Discipline of the Church; care being taken to adhere as much as possible to the relative proportions of such a structure.

The principle indeed of sacred associations of this nature comes to us with the very highest authority, by the constant use of it throughout the whole of Scripture, from the Tabernacle in the Wilderness, which served for an "example and shadow of heavenly things," to the fuller application and extensive unfoldings of the same symbolical figures in the book of the Revelation. And, indeed, the practice is hallowed to us by the use of our Lord Himself, Who, from the pouring out of water on the great day of the Feast of

Tabernacles, took occasion to speak of the Holy Ghost, and likened a door (presented to their eyes as is supposed in the precincts of the Temple) to Himself; and made bread, and the water of the well, significative emblems of things heavenly and divine. And indeed, if we may say it with reverence, it was the very characteristic of our Lord's teaching, to draw moral and religious instruction from visible objects.

*The Eve of the Annunciation,*
    1838.

# CONTENTS.

## PART II.

### *THE NAVE.*

## PART III.

### *THE CHOIR.*

## PART IV.

### *THE PILLARS AND WINDOWS.*

### THE PILLARS.

## THE WINDOWS.

# THE DEDICATION.

THOU Who Thy tabernacle mad'st of old
 To be a type of things invisible,
 And didst within Thy temple come to dwell
Making it holy ; I Thine altar hold,
And pray Thee, if such prayer be not too bold,
 To sanctify each shrine, and mystic cell
 Round this Thine altar, and baptismal well.
Thou vilest things to Thy great ends dost mould : —
 Accept this offering, and Thy servant spare,
 Who this hath built with sin-defiled hands !
 And when Thine earthly Temple, now so fair
Among the things that have gone by shall be,
 And nothing but Thy heavenly Temple stands,
Pity me in that day, in that day pity me !
And ye that enter at this Temple-gate,
 When your full hearts ye in His presence pour
 Think of an unclean leper at the door,
Admitted erst to your high-gifted state,
But by unhallow'd taints left desolate !
 And Thou who intercedest for the poor,
 Within Thine unseen Temple evermore,
Plead for his pardon ere it be too late.
 Thou didst the leper touch, and take his sin :
 Heal his sick soul, that he may entrance win
 To Thy blest City, and so gain within
Thy Priestly Absolution while he may,
Lest he be laid without too late to pray,
When once the Judge hath risen, and clos'd the door for aye.

# PART I.

# The Exterior of the Cathedral.

———

## THE APPROACH.

*When all the air calm Evening woos,*
  *And earthly mists are wafted by,*
  *And nought unholy breathing nigh,*
*Yon grove in deeps of its repose*
*A wondrous portal doth disclose,*
  *And far within a living way,*
  *Lit up by an unfading day,*
*Thro' the long gloomy vale of woes.*
*And child-like Wisdom holds the key,*
  *And Wealth, that to the world is poor,*
  *Wide opes to them that ivory door,*
*Where all in other colours stand,*
*Touch'd by a disenchanting wand,*
*And things that seem'd of earth, of Heaven are found to be.*

Open to me the gates of righteousness, that I may go into them,
and give thanks unto the Lord.

# The Western Front.

| LEFT HAND DOOR. | MIDDLE DOOR. | RIGHT HAND DOOR. |
| REPENTANCE. | OBEDIENCE. | FAITH. |

## Baptismal Promises.

This is the gate of the Lord : the righteous shall enter into it.

PSALM cxviii. 19, 20.

# The Western Front.

BAPTISMAL PROMISES.

## The Left-hand Door.

### *Repentance.*

REPENTANCE is the lowly door,
That leads to yon baptismal well,
Which hath its source where Angels dwell :
Thence many an arching aisle doth soar,
Thence stretches many a sacred floor,
And many a thought-inspiring cell,
Peopling our sacred citadel :
At that blest fountain evermore,
Calm Faith, and holy Hope doth spring,
And Prayer bedews her wearied wing :
There many a bright and Angel guest,
With varied plume and changeful vest,
Shall lead thee on, and thence shall bring
To God's own mount, thy place of rest.

### II.

But this no home for Fancy deem,
Still Morn and Evening, o'er and o'er,
Thou must stoop through the lowly door,
Still wilt thou at the threshold seem,
Still but awakening from the dream ;
For what though Jordan's stream be past,
The Canaanite is gathering fast :
Still as thou travellest in the beam
Of that new morning, more and more
Thou shalt thy sinful self deplore :
Thy worldly wisdom still unlearning,
Still to a Father's house returning,
In lights of that celestial store,
Thine image lost the more discerning.

## III.

So daily mayst thou less become
  In thine own eyes, and thus beguil'd
   Into the likeness of a child,
The narrow gate shall give thee room :
As dawns the light of thy last home,
  The wreaths of Eden, sin-defil'd,
  Drop off, but thou art reconcil'd
To sorrow, leaving some, and some
Before thee gone, and waiting thee,
  Where relics of lost Paradise
  Are gathering ; thus made lowly wise,
Till Life's dark porch shall set thee free,
  And there shall break upon thine eyes
The temple of Eternity.

## The Middle Door.

*Obedience.*

IF thou art one whose cry is Liberty,
  Pass not the portal of our hallow'd shrine,
We in a holier freedom would be free.
  If thou in wealth or honour lov'st to shine,
  To build in cedars, or at ease recline,
No holy awe thy tongue and foot shall hold
  In those lov'd haunts, where ancient Discipline
Keeps watch, amid her treasures manifold,
And welcomes to stern walls and dim cathedrals old.


### II.

At her command the Apostolic key
  Opens the solemn doors, in speaking stone
Her glories far withdraw, where none can see,
  Seeking the Infinite in secret known,
  And tell of wonders which surround His throne ;
Her carv'd embroideries, which retire aloof,
  Are ancient virtues, seen by God alone,
And His good Angels, mysteries learn'd by proof,
And prayers which hide from man o'er Heaven's embower-
    ing roof.


### III.

Ye cloistral shades, and angel-haunted cells,
  Chantries, and tuneful roofs, and Altars old,
Where incommunicable Godhead dwells !
  Let your dread spirit fill me, my hand hold,
  And every thought to your obedience mould
While through the avenue of number'd years,
  As through a pillar'd vista, I behold
Where Christ for me the bleeding burden bears,
Till all my heart be love, and soul-constraining fears ;

## IV.

And I learn your deep lesson, up that road
    To Calvary's awful mount Thy Cross to bear,
After Thee and with Thee, and share Thy load ;—
    Divine prerogative ! if so brought near,
    And made in that similitude more dear,
We share too Thine Anointing ; heart and knee
    Shall so gain firmness, till in holier fear,
Clinging beneath the foot of that dread Tree,
We hide ourselves, and look, dear Lord, to Thee,

## V.

Calm on the Rock of Ages.   While below,
    For ever restless and for ever loud,
Toss the tumultuous seas of human woe,
    Death and decay, like shadows of a cloud,
    Pass o'er each scene, and if we be allow'd
To linger on, like waves which break on waves,
    All that we lov'd to dim destruction crowd ;
Day and Night swifter seek their silent caves,
And we are left alone, standing above our graves,

## VI.

Which are the mouths of that unfathom'd sea,
    Whose awful secrets Thou alone canst tell !
Then where flee we for refuge, but to Thee,
    And Thine obedience ? heaven-constructed cell,
    Wherein, as in a temple, Love doth dwell,
While tempests war around, with suppliant eyes
    To penitential prayer composed well,
Awaiting, till the Day-spring shall arise,
And with the Judgment ope the everlasting skies.

## The Right-hand Door.

### Faith.

A WANDERER thro' the vale of years,
  And westward bent her pilgrim feet,
  Here Faith hath made her last retreat.
A wondrous key her shoulder bears,
The blue of Heaven the stole she wears :
  When Angels left sad Eden's seat,
  She stay'd, fall'n man's companion meet ;
Again his downcast head she rears,
    And seeks the lost to bear their woes ;
  'Twas she at Jordan[1] vigils kept,
  And by Euphrates[2] sat and wept :—
To them who will her secret prove
    A hidden cross she doth disclose,
A word that may the mountains move.


### II.

Here now the Church's pillar'd shrine
  She hath her habitation made,
  And sanctified the solemn shade ;
Bidding celestial brightness shine,
Where else were but a formless mine.
  When these dead walls her heaven-born aid,
  And secret spirit shall pervade,
Terrestrial things become divine :
    'Tis on her breath the Collect soars,
    And Psalms attain the eternal doors ;
  No health in the baptismal wave,
  In hallowed cup no power to save,
Without her—Life a cheerless noon,
And Death a night without a moon.

[1 Josh. iii. 17.]        [2 Ps. cxxxvii. 1.]

### III.

Here when her rapt eye heavenward streams
  In calm and holy Litanies,
  She bringeth down the pitying skies ;
The dove upon the fountain gleams,
In broad mysterious blessing teems.
  Thence going forth she to chaste eyes
  Clothes Nature with her sympathies ;
When night's dark curtains fall, she seems
    On mountain tops with silvery feet,
    Holding with Heaven communion sweet ;
  When clouds Heaven's moving surface wield,
  She opes beyond her bright-blue shield ;
When warring tumults gather near,
She lifts the consecrated spear.

Thou shalt hide them privily by Thine own presence from the
provoking of all men.

# The Cloisters.

## ECCLESIASTICAL SONNETS.

Thou shalt keep them secretly in Thy tabernacle from the strife of
tongues.

PSALM xxxi. 20.

# The Cloisters.

## ECCLESIASTICAL SONNETS.

### I.

### *The Liturgy.*

Ask for the old paths, where is the good way, and walk therein, and
ye shall find rest.

A PATH of peace amid the tangled grove,
   A moon-lit way of sweet security—
   Bright holy days that form a galaxy
To make a road to Heaven—strains from above
Whereon the spheres of duty kindlier move,
   Drinking pure light and heaven-born harmony—
   Such is the path of thy calm Liturgy,
Ancient of mothers, in parental love
   Daily unwinding from thine annual maze
   Treasures that wax not old, whence still may grow
Fresh adoration.   On thy face (of thee
   Praying to be more worthy) as we gaze
   Thy soul comes forth in beauty, and thy brow
So calm, is full of holiest Deity.

## II.

### *Forms.*

The care of discipline is love.

LOVE, from whatever earthly cave he springs,
 (That spell of something heavenly dwelling round
 Home, friend, or grave endear'd,) when he hath found
Meet entrance, he will shake his odorous wings,
And throw a charm o'er thousand meaner things,
 O'er whatsoe'er at first he entrance found
 Into the soul ; in ties associate bound
He lives, and o'er them his own radiance flings.
 Then why should not a holier Peace and Mirth
 Love those mute forms, which cherish'd first their birth,
 And brac'd them for the withering blasts of earth ?
The gladsome soul that her devotion plies,
Bound in the wreath of ancient Liturgies,
Why should she not her chain beyond all freedom prize ?

## III.

### *The Collect for the Day.*

They will go from strength to strength.

AND let me, loving still of thee to learn,
Thy weekly Collect on my spirit wear,
That so my steps may turn to practice clear,
And 'scape those ways where feverish fancies burn ;
So may thy Sunday thoughts at every turn
   Meet us, like healthful founts in Elim green,[1]
   Casting a freshness o'er the week.  This scene
Of outward things, as still the wheels return,
Leads sternly to decay : thou ever true,
   As on the grave and withering age we gain,[2]
Thy tale of better things dost still renew,
   Like tune that pleas'd our childhood's pensive ear
   Still as we older grow 'tis doubly dear,
Aye wakening echoes new, and deep and deeper strain.

---

[1] Exodus xv. 27.
[2] "Gain," in the sense of overtaking, "As in the race we draw ever closer to this grave," &c.  The last lines appear to be suggested by a well-known stanza in the opening poem of the *Christian Year.*]

## IV.

### *Prayer.*

They shall be satisfied with the pleasures of Thy house, even of
Thy holy temple.

HIDDEN, exhaustless treasury, heaven-taught Prayer,
  Armoury of unseen aids—watchword and spell
  At which blest Angels pitch their tent and dwell
About us—glass to bring the bright Heavens near—
Sea of eternal beauty—wondrous stair
  By patriarch seen—key leading to a cell
  Where better worlds are hidden—secret well
Where Love with golden chalice may repair,
  And slake his thirst, nursing with fragrant dews
Heaven's lilies fair, and rose on wild-wood spray,
Calm thought and high resolve ! strange instrument,
  Wherewith from spheres serene Music is sent
  Into the mind, throwing o'er all fresh hues,
And mystic colourings—yet we cannot pray !

[This exquisite sonnet is full of Scriptural allusions : Eph. vi. 18 ;
2 Kings vi. 17 ; Rev. iv. 6 ; Gen. xxviii. 12.]

## V.

### *The Complaint.*

Lord, who shall dwell in Thy tabernacle, or who shall rest on
Thy holy hill?

WE cannot pray, strange mystery ! here is known
 No wearying—no deceivings. of sick Hope,
 No aching limb, or brow, wherewith to cope—
No pallid after-thoughts—and of the boon
No half-surmis'd upbraiding—no cold frown
 Bidding us come again—no lengthening slope ·
 Tiring the eye from far.  These portals ope
To dwellings lucid as th' autumnal moon,
But we along the world's slow sluggish strand
 Are fostering vanity, which joint by joint
Climbs, like Nile's[1] reed, into a tufted crown,
And woos each wind that waves its golden down ;
 All hollow, soon a barbed shaft 'twill point,
Or staff, to pierce light heart or trusting hand.

[[1] Allusion to 2 Kings xviii. 21.  The *arundo donax* is the plant
alluded to.  See a picture of it in Smith's *Dictionary of the Bible*,
*s.v.* " Reed."]

## VI.

*Sunday.*

This is the day which the Lord hath made ; we will rejoice
and be glad in it.

Sweet day, let not the clouds of earthly Care
    Come over thy calm brightness, let Reproof
    And pale Remorse and Sadness stand aloof,
Let nought of worldly strife, or ruder air,
Ruffle, or rend the mantle thou dost wear !
    The robe thou wear'st is all celestial woof,
    Come from the grave with Jesus.   Heaven's blue roof
Seems nearer earth, and all earth hath of fair
Is fairer.   On thy calm and glassy floor
    We sit in commune sweet, thy riches blest
Recounting, and forget that we are poor.
    Let us be bright to meet thee, Angel guest,
    With contemplations of enduring rest,
And with thee listen at the heavenly door.

## VII.

*Village Psalmody.*

All my fresh springs shall be in thee.

AND is it not thy praise, Church of our love,
     That thou unto each little rural nook
     Of quiet hast soft golden plumage shook
From off the wing of thine own David's dove,
And turn'd the melodies, that nearest prove
     To the heart of man, into a sacred book,—
     Key to the soul's best avenues,—a brook
That steals into Religion's secret grove?
     If those straw roofs and ivied cots among
There play a gleam of song, 'tis no wild fire,
But sparks, tho' scatter'd, from a heaven-strung lyre.
     Thus, when the cloud of music roll'd along
Fills the melodious dome, blest sounds inspire
     Each cloistral nook, vocal with sacred song.

## VIII.

### *The ancient Village.*

And the daughter of Zion is left as a cottage in a vineyard.

LET me still love thee in thy quietude,
　　Sweet sylvan village ! and thou, aged rook,
　　Who sitt'st sole sentinel in ivied nook,
Survivor of thy noisy brotherhood !
And I with thee, in thine own pensive mood,
　　Could linger, till the lights of ages fall
　　Around us, like moonbeams on tap'stried hall,
And saintly forms come forth, and virgins good,
　　Who gave their days to Heaven.　From that lone pile
Avaunt,[1] rude change, thy disenchanting wand,
　　And let the holy Cross linger awhile !
　　Ah, feather'd Chronicler, would that from thee
Thou couldst forefend Art's all-transforming hand,
　　And guard thy hoary haunts of sweet Antiquity.

[1 This is a harsh expression.　"Avaunt" is an interjection ; our author uses it as if it were a transitive verb governing "wand."]

## IX.

### *The modern Cathedral.*

Ye have said, It is vain to serve God ; and what profit is it that we
have kept His ordinances ?

WITHOUT—the world's unceasing noises rise,
Turmoil, disquietude, and busy fears.
Within—there are the sounds of other years,
Thoughts full of Prayer, and solemn harmonies,
Which imitate on earth the peaceful skies,
  And canonized Regret, which backward bears
  Her longing aspect, moving thoughtful tears.
Such blest abodes, in Heaven's all-pitying eyes,
  Might yet be eloquent for a nation's good ;
  But where is now the kneeling multitude ?
The silver-tongued spruce verger passes by
Hurrying his group, the proud and curious eye
  Of connoisseur—the loiterer's sauntering mood :
Sad picture of lost Faith and evil nigh !

[We may thankfully trust that since this sonnet was written, the Church
has come to realise better the proper functions of our Cathedrals.]

## X.

### *The Daily Service.*

Where two or three are gathered together in My Name, there am I in the midst of them.

AND are we then alone on holy ground,
　　Most gracious Father?　Are we then alone,
　　Because the world regards not, and is gone?
Where are the solemn dead which lie around,
Are they not with us?　Are Thy courts not crown'd
　　With spiritual hosts about, while the sweet tone
　　Still lingers round Thine Altars?　Are they flown,
Bearing no more to see their God disown'd?
Has the great Michael left us, mighty arm,
　　Gabriel, our fortitude, and the blest charm
Of Raphael's healing name?[1]　In my heart's fear
　　I heard a voice, " Be still, and lowly bend ;
While two or three remain, thy Lord is here,
　　And where His presence is, His Hosts attend."

[1 The name means " The Divine Healer."　According to one Jewish tradition he was one of the five angels standing by the throne of God, and to him was committed the work of healing the schism of the two kingdoms.　He appears in the Book of Tobit as the deliverer of Sara from her plague, and of Tobit from blindness.]

## XI.

### *Foreign Breviaries.*

They that worship Him shall worship Him in spirit and in truth.

DEAR Church, our island's sacred sojourner,
 A richer dress thy Southern sisters own,
 And some would deem too bright their flowing zone
For sacred walls. I love thee, nor would stir
Thy simple note, severe in character,
 By use made lovelier, for the lofty tone
 Of hymn, response, and touching antiphone,
Lest we lose homelier truth. The chorister
That sings the summer nights, so soft and strong,
 To music modulating his sweet throat,
 Labours with richness of his varied note,
Yet lifts not unto Heaven a holier song,
 Than our home bird that, on some leafless thorn,
 Hymns his plain chaunt each wintry eve and morn.

[Dr Newman's celebrated Tract (*Tracts for the Times*, No. 75) "On the Roman Breviary," was published in July 1836, and evidently suggested the above poem.]

## XII.

### *The Church in Scotland.*

Rejoice not against me, O mine enemy ; when I fall, I shall arise ;
when I sit in darkness, the Lord shall be a light unto me.

MORE pure the gale where the wild thistle rears
  His mountain banner on his stony tower,
  Than odorous breath of cultivated bower ;
More true to nature o'er its armed spears
The mountain rose its lonely chalice bears,
  Than many-folding cups of cherish'd flower ;
  And, traversing those wilds with silvery shower,
E'en Winter's moon more clear and free appears !
  Such is thy sister of the northern hills,
  Less honour'd, not less holy ; bow'd with ills,
But not destroy'd ; pure branch of the true vine,
  Drinking her nurture from the barren rock,
  Of pitiless elements she braves the shock,
And hath less earthly beauty—more divine.

[The death of the saintly Bishop Jolly in 1837, the year before *The Cathedral* was published, had caused wide regret, and had called much attention to the Episcopal Church of Scotland. One result was the calling of a General Synod in August 1838, and the formation of the "Scottish Episcopal Church Society," to forward the work of the Church. One of the original Vice-Presidents was Mr Gladstone. See Lawson's "History of the Scottish Episcopal Church," p. 400.]

## XIII.

### *The Church in Wales.*

Why hast thou broken down her hedges, that all they that go by pluck
off her grapes?

ALAS, Menevia! what of thee remains,
    Primeval saintly Church? from Towy's flood
    To Conway springs an ever teeming brood
Of novelty, to claim thy true domains;
Religious Freedom, worse than Romish chains!
    As in the stool where some huge oak once stood
    Some mountain bird now hides his sylvan food;
And lo! the ancient stock with wonder gains
A doubtful, new, and motley progeny,
    Springing in mockery from her aged root,
    With coral berries wild and show of fruit.
    And here and there between, the ancestral shoot
Is seen to emulate their pliancy,
Bowing to each wind as it passes by.

## XIV.

### *The Church in Wales.*

Wherefore, when I looked that it should bring forth grapes,
brought it forth wild grapes?'

ANCIENT Menevia, I must still love thee,
  Nor yet is silent thy Cathedral song,
  Though nought to echo back her solemn tongue,
Save the true emblems of Heaven's constancy,
Th' unchanging mountains and unchanging Sea,
  Which to each other thy deep tones prolong,
  And both bear on to Heaven.   What though, among
Thine innocent nuptial feasts and household glee,
  Thy harp is silenc'd in Religion's name,
  And Discipline become a word of blame,
Mother of love and nurse of cheerful thought,
While holiest liturgies are set at nought,
  To enshrine the feverish dreams of human will,
  Ancient Menevia, I must love thee still.

.

.

## XV.

### *The Church in Wales.*

Turn Thee again, Thou Lord of hosts, look down from Heaven,
 behold, and visit this vine.

FOR thou didst take me up unto thy breast,
  Pitying my lost and helpless infancy,
  And didst engraft me in the living tree.
Still breathe fresh thoughts from thy Plinlimmon's crest.
Hedg'd by thy language, (in thy mountain-nest,
  Indented oft with blue o'er-arching sea,)
  That so the airs of foul disloyalty
Reach thee but faintly from our sad unrest,
  Which, like Avernian steams, to Heaven's deep roof
  Daily ascend, and gathering there aloof,
Hang in tempestuous clouds.   If thou wouldst still
  Have thy good Angel guard thee free from blame,
Rend not Christ's robe at thine irreverent will,
  But wrap it round thee, lest they see thy shame.

## XVI.

### *Political Changes.*

I have seen an end of all perfection, but Thy commandment
is exceeding broad.

Strange—the o'erwhelming tide that beareth on
  The soul of Nations—mighty, though unseen,
  And wielding mighty destinies ; not e'en
Huge Ocean, on his bed with thunder strewn,
Rocking from pole to pole to the pale Moon,
  More constant in mutation ; 'mid the scene
  We stretch our sounding canvas, nor aught ween
Our whereabouts, save where the past hath gone !
  It was the Everlasting that pass'd by,
We saw not, but in cloud o'er cloud array'd,
  Ocean o'er ocean roll'd ineffably,
  Onward, like tide-born billows, He doth heave
Men's spirits, each upon his own bark staid.
  We to behold His Glory's skirts had leave.

See Introduction, p. 7.]

## XVII.

### *The sure Covenant.*

For this is as the waters of Noah unto Me; for as I have sworn the
    waters shall no more go over the earth, so have I sworn that I
    would not be wroth with thee.

LET the storms ply their deep and threatening bass,
    The Bow of Promise shall the shades illume,
Brightly descried in Faith's eternal glass,
    E'en like an Angel's many-colour'd plume
    Waving in tempest—pledge that in her bloom
Nature, emerging from the stormy mass,
Will keep her time and order,—Let them pass,
    The wicked and their plottings : mid the gloom,
The Church surveys her Covenant sign, and smiles.
    And 'neath her solemn rainbow's dripping arch,
    A mystic wing spread o'er her daring march,
She goes forth, on her heavenly work the whiles,
    Though weeping, sure that One in joy shall bring
    Her and her sheaves at harvest-moon to sing.

## XVIII.

### *Prayer for the Parliament.*

God forbid that I should sin against the Lord, in ceasing to
pray for you.

YET Peace be in these walls !   Upon them rest
  The Royal Martyr's mantle from the skies,[1]
  Though little they Heaven's sweet protection prize !
And haply so our prayers to our own breast
Unanswer'd may return, yet not unblest,
  If thus our soul learn patience, and arise,
  Good CHARLES, to thy diviner charities !
Albeit oft, with heavy thoughts opprest,
  We see in them but clouds from our sick land,
  And the dread sword unsheath'd in God's right hand.
Thus set we the soul's anchor, if it be
  Right in th' All-seeing eyes, then be it so,
May the vex'd Church learn her true panoply,
  And lift above the clouds her tranquil brow.

This Prayer was appointed in the reign of King Charles the First.

## XIX.

*Prayer for the King.*

Honour thy father and thy mother, that thy days may be long.

IF the meek-hearted to the earth is heir,
   Refresh'd in multitude of peace divine,
   And length of days, by what blest discipline
Shall we best drink of that celestial air?
By what calm ways of holy Wisdom share
   Th' eternal sweetness of her Angel eyne,
   Who leans on high from the meek Saviour's shrine?
The path of Life will shew—the path of Prayer.
   There filial duty first shall lead thee by
   The house of Pride, then manhood's Loyalty
Take thee in hand, her spirit to infuse.
Pray thou with them, imbibe their heavenly hues,
And they will lead thee to that Palace Hall,
Where God is King and Father, all in all.

## XX.

### *Consolations of Baptism.*

O Israel, thou hast destroyed thyself, but in Me is thy help.

BRIGHTLY the Morn of our New Birth arose
  From the Baptismal Fount, in awful trance
  Unveiling half her glorious countenance ;
We turn'd to our own dreams, wooing Earth's woes,
And slumber'd.  Haply now ere Ev'ning's close
  We wake, and o'er us see a pitying glance,
  The heavenly morn gone by, day in advance,
And far away the towers of our repose.
  We doubt the title soil'd by sinful stain,
  And of our birthright ask some sign again,
Such is distrust, of Sin the penalty !
  Oh ! rather, when thy knees sink on the plain,
Rise, and look back on that Egyptian sea,
  And doubt no more the arm that set thee free.

## XXI.

### *The City of God.* [1]

Glorious things are spoken of thee, thou City of God.

THROUGHOUT the older word, story and rite—
    Throughout the new, skirting all clouds with gold—
    Through rise and fall and destinies manifold
Of pagan empires—through the dreams and night
Of nature, and the darkness and the light,
    Still young in hope, in disappointment old—
    Through mists which fall'n humanity enfold—
Into the vast and viewless infinite,
    Rises th' Eternal City of our God.
    Her towers the morn with disenchanting rod
Dimly and darkly·labours to disclose,
    Lifting the outskirts of the o'er-mantling gloom ;
    Bright shapes come forth, arch, pinnacle, and dome,
In Heaven is hid its height and deep repose.

[1] On reading St Augustine's *De Civitate Dei.*

## XXII.

### *New Ways.*

Then is the offence of the Cross ceased.

Now each new Creed will ready welcome move,[1]
   That bids not in the secret soul to bear
   The Cross with Thee, in silence and in fear,
And Duty's silvery trappings yoked with Love.
O sternly kind Severity, to prove
   The children of the promise, year by year,
   And that unearthly bosom calm and clear,
Meet mirror to enshrine th' Eternal Dove.
Yet this is hard—this holy:[2] turn thine eyes
   Inward, and thou shalt find the broad new way,
Like the foul Stygian deep, where hideous things
Stable in darkness, and but fold their wings
   Deeming it light—be thine to fear and pray,
And feed on that life-giving Sacrifice !

[1 Every Creed will win a chance of welcome which does not exhort
men to bear the cross.]
[2 But this holiness is a hard road to travel; the broad way of the
natural man is easier.]

## XXIII.

### *The Crucifix.*

That I may know Him, and the fellowship of His sufferings, being
made conformable unto His death.

THOUGH by such thorns as on Thy brow abide,[1]
  Thine would Thy servant be—thorns from the weed
  Of sorrow, whereof Adam sowed the seed ;
Thine by the spear that pierced Thy tender side,
Compunctuous throes, which drink the heart's deep tide ;
  Thine by the nails, which made Thy pure hands bleed,—
  Nails of stern discipline, rough arts that breed
Keen penitential yearnings, or the pride
Of the rude scoffing world ; by whate'er chain
  May quell rebellion or of soul or eye,
Whatever penance schools[2] of shame, or pain,
Whatever scourge may strike, and not in vain,
  So bind me to Thy Cross, that I may die
Daily, the fleeting years that I remain.

[1] I would fain be Thy servant, even though it be by thorns and
discipline, &c.]
[2] Schools, *i.e.*, teaches.]

## XXIV.

### *The Holy Altar.*

The glory of the Lord came into the house by the way of the gate,
whose prospect is toward the East.

*UNTO the East we turn*, to which belong
   More than the heart divines, or eye descries ;
   There is the Altar which our life supplies.
The voice is silent, lest it should do wrong
To things which are too high for mortal tongue.
   The Heavens are looking on with wondering eyes,
   And Angel faces crowd the o'erhanging skies.
Shall men unheeding to the temple throng
   Where God is present ?   Watchful evermore,
Let calm Obeisance at Thine Altar wait,
   And lowly-bowing Reverence keep the door
  Of our dull hearts ; that there we may be brought
  To the society of holy thought,
Revering God, to man compassionate.

## XXV.

### *The Ancient Church.*

I will lift up mine eyes unto the hills, from whence cometh my help.

*UNTO the East we turn*—from the cold bourn
  Of our dull western cave Faith's pensive mood
  Sets there her tranced eyelid, gathering food
Of solemn thoughts which make her less forlorn,
And back to Apostolic men is borne.
  There, from her evening and dim solitude,
  She joins the companies of the wise and good,
Who walk upon the Gospel's glorious morn,
  Their dwarf dimensions of mortality
  Seeming to grow upon the golden sky,
Beyond the cold shade of imperious Rome.
  Ambrose and Basil, either Gregory,[1]
Clement and Cyril, Cyprian's earthly home,
And the free lips of glowing Chrysostom.

[[1] The two Gregories, Thaumaturgus and Nazianzen.]

## XXVI.

### *The Holy Land.*

His windows being open in his chamber towards Jerusalem, he
kneeled upon his knees and prayed.

*UNTO the East we turn*—like some bright stair
  Let down from Heaven, the land where Angels still
  Linger at Chinnereth's lake or Tabor's hill.
Here Jesus sat, there stood, here kneel'd in prayer ;
Here was His cradle, there His sepulchre.
  E'en now appears the bleeding spectacle
  Upheld to the wide world : the cup of ill
Is drain'd, with hands outstretch'd, bleeding and bare,
He doth in death His innocent head recline,
  Turn'd to the West.   Descending from his height,
  The sun beheld, and veil'd Him from the sight.
Thither, while from the serpent's wound we pine,
To Thee, remembering that baptismal sign,
  We turn, and drink anew Thy healing might.

## XXVII.

### *Lost Eden.*

When they return unto Thee, in the land of their enemies, and pray
unto Thee toward their land which Thou gavest unto their fathers,
then hear Thou their supplication in Heaven.

*UNTO the East we turn*, in thoughtful gaze,
   Like longing exiles to their ancient home,
   Mindful of our lost Eden. Thence may come
Genial ambrosial airs around the ways
Of daily life, and fragrant thoughts that raise
   Home-sympathies : so may we cease to roam,
   Seeking some resting-place before the tomb,
To which on wandering wings devotion strays.
   But true to our high birthright, and to Him
   Who leads us by the flaming Cherubim,
Death's gate, our pilgrim spirits may arise
   O'er earth's affections ; and 'mid worldlings rude,
   Walk loosely in their holier solitude,
And breathe the air of their lost Paradise.

## XXVIII.

### *The Coming of Christ.*

As the lightning cometh out of the East, and shineth even unto the
West, so shall also the coming of the Son of Man be.

*Unto the East we turn,* with watchful eyes,
    Where opens the white haze of silvery lawn,
    And the still trees stand in the streak of dawn,
Until the Sun of Righteousness shall rise,
And far behind shall open all the skies,
    And golden clouds of Angels be withdrawn
    Around His presence.   Then there shall be gone,
Fleeing before His face in dread surprise,
    The Heaven and Earth and the affrighted Sea,
And the tribunal shall be set on high,
    And we the fiery trial must abide.
Like nightly travellers to the kindling sky,
    Awake or sleeping to yon eastern side
    We turn, and know not when the time shall be.

## The Way to the Chapter-house.

### *Sacred Retirement.*

A MOUNTAIN lake, where sleeps the mid-day Moon,
　　When beetle booming by is heard no more—
'Twixt drowsy hills and sea a sultry noon—
　　A rural Church, some evening funeral o'er—
　　A leaf's still image in a fountain hoar—
On cloistral pane the gaze of Saint or Seer,
　　Suffus'd with lessons sweet of heavenly lore,
And heavenly-rapt affection—These all wear
Calm unalloy'd, but none so deep as lingereth here.

### II.

The long green avenue, where light and shade
　　Chequering the floor, now play, now sleep profound ;
Old pines, the lonely breeze that by them stray'd
　　Wooing in vain ; old yews, hiding the ground,
　　Grey oaks, and far-off spires, seem to have found
A voice, while busier sounds are dimly spent,
　　As waken'd by the stillness.　One around,
On pillars of blue light hath spread His tent ;
And walks with us below in silence eloquent.

### III.

And now we hear Him : thus when Nature's wheel
　　Is still, we find ourselves hurrying along ;
In crowds ourselves alone we mostly feel ;
　　When turbulence of business, and the throng
　　Of passionate hopes, which unto Earth belong,

And mould too oft from Earth the rebel will,
    Sleep ;—then we hear the mighty undersong,
To which loud Niagara's voice is still,
And mute the thunders strong which air and ocean fill.


## IV.

O heavenly Love, that o'er us, sin defil'd,
    With thy blest arm beneath us, leaning low,
Dost watch, fond mother, o'er thy slumbering child,
    That still in dreams is tossing to and fro,
    And knowing knows thee not ! Aye come and go
Thy messengers of pity ; from Heaven's door
    The star its silver image shoots below,
Seen instantaneous in the wat'ry floor ;
So quick 'tween Earth and Heaven thy beams of mercy pour !


## V.

Into my cold and leaden spirit stream,
    Out of thy Star of beauty, that doth burn
Around my Saviour's brow ! O grant one beam,
    One faint, dim emanation from thine urn,
    Which e'en in me may so responsive turn,
Like magnet to thy pole, that I may rove
    No longer.   I my daily path would earn,
And gather tow'rd the haven ; I would move
On by thy light till lost in everlasting love.


## VI.

Oh ! hide me in thy temple, ark serene,
    Where safe upon the swell of this rude sea,
I might survey the stars, thy towers between,
    And might pray always ; not that I would be
    Uplifted, or would fain not dwell with thee
On the rough waters, but in soul within
    I sigh for thy pure calm, serene and free ;
I too would prove thy Temple, 'mid the din
Of earthly things, unstain'd by care or sin !

## VII.

Into the deeps, where Ev'ning holds her court,
    A feather'd flock are winging their wild flight,
Now gradual fading far, now borne athwart,
    And seen again, now lost in Infinite
    And Sea of purple ; we, with eager sight
Would match their soaring wings, as on the swell
    Of music, ling'ring in some vaulted height,—
Then sink, and feel our chain and earthly cell ;—
When shall the soul be free, and in those glories dwell !

He that entereth in by the door is the shepherd of the sheep.

# The Chapter-House.

## EPISCOPACY.

Verily, verily, I say unto you, I am the door of the sheep.

St John x. 2, 7.

## The Chapter-house.

*Episcopacy.*

I. *The Key-stone of the visible Church.*  II. *Sacred antiquity.*  III.
*Divine Commission.*  IV. *Enmity of the world.*  V. *Its power spiritual.*
VI. *Its blessings.*  VII. *Its dress Humility.*  VIII. *Succession from
the Apostles.*

---

The Presbytery, being worthy of God, is united to the Bishop, as the
strings are to an harp, thus bound together in union of heart and voice,
and in that love of which Jesus Christ is the Leader and the Guardian.
—*Ignatius' Epist. to the Ephesians*, c. iv.

## I.

MYSTERIOUS harp of heaven-born harmony !
 Touch'd by th' all-hallowing Spirit from above,
 Thou fill'st the Church, else dead, with duteous love,
Obedience, such as holds the hosts on high,
And pure heaven-soothing order.   Mortal eye
  Beholds not, nor can mortal hearing prove
  The musical soul which on thy chords doth move,
Tempering to holiest union ; but the sky
  May catch the echo of the unearthly sound,
For Christ Himself, and His appointed few,
  Moulded the frame, and in the silvery bound
Set all the glowing wires.   Then potent grew
  (Like that pale starry lyre 'twixt sea and cloud
  Seen fitfully in Heaven when winds are loud)
The treasury of sweet sounds : deep aisle and fane
Prolong, from age to age, the harmonious strain.

## II.

The soul that knows not thy constraining power,
 Sacred Antiquity ! hath lost a spell
 From Heaven,—a delicate chain impalpable
To hold clear spirits ; he hath miss'd the tower
Where Faith finds refuge, marr'd the sacred flower
  Of bloom and modesty, aye wont to dwell
  On Virtue's awful face.   Love hath a cell
Where, watch'd and treasur'd as her choicest dower,

She keeps what bears the impress of her Lord,
Now doubly dear by age ; such high control
  Is Piety's life-breath.  If Freedom's word
 Finds in thy breast an echo, lay aside
That right-asserting attitude of soul,
  Ere in the Christian's temple thou abide,
Where he who dwells must dwell on bended knee,
From his own merits praying to be free.

### III.

The Sovereignty of God is shed o'er Kings,
  Throwing around them a mysterious fear,
  Which, though it would not, cannot but revere,
When the true Line, in type of heavenly things,
The shadow of God's Kingship o'er them flings.
  But in Thy Priesthood Thou Thyself art here,
  And virtue goeth from Thee.  Faith brings near
That heaven-descended stair, and upward springs,
  With world-averted face, and, more and more,
  Admitting to Thy Godhead's secret store,
Leads up to Thee.  Healing Thy garments fills,
And grace and truth th' impregnate air distils
  Around thy presence.  With awe-stricken eyes
We sit with lov'd disciples round Thy feet ;
  Or, as the growing bread Thy love supplies,
From Apostolic hands we take and eat.

### IV.

The Persian king,[1] from arm'd Abdera's rocks,
  Fetter'd and lash'd free Ocean ; who the while,
  Not to o'erwhelm him, with a patient smile,
Forbore to shake his spray-bespangled locks :
'Tis thus when man the Almighty's goodness mocks ;—
  The chosen of the vineyard rose, and said,
  Come, let us kill the Heir ; when He is dead
All will be ours.  The world is bold, and shocks
  Our boasted reason ; yet from age to age
Proud scorners play that descant o'er and o'er :
  When the world's minions, or in mirth or rage,
  Lifting the scourge o'er crown or shrine, engage,

[1 Xerxes, who had the sea scourged, and fetters thrown into it, because a storm had scattered his fleet. Herod. vi. 35.]

These be my spoils, these only, and no more,
The Church, forbearing, as that sea forbore,
    Moves not to crush, but careless of the chain,
    Looks bright, and breathes out her untroubled strain.

### V.

Welcome their hate; the good which they dispense
    Poisons the proud and pains the lowly soul;
    Nor can the spells which this rude world control,
And worldly arts, and wit, and eloquence,
One spirit rescue from the toils of sense,
    Or bring one rescued to the eternal goal.
    Thy robe must be thy Master's humble stole,[1]
Watching and fast, and fast and watching, thence
    Long midnight meditations, grave and deep,
    Rous'd from earth's palsying hand of drowsy sleep
By Persecution's wrath and Satan's hate,
And wafting prayers of saints that on thee wait,
    Some Herbert[2] hidden in his rural nook,
    Or Kempis[3] kneeling o'er a cloistral book,
And chief of spells, the halo yet unspent,
The latest breath of Jesus ere he went.[4]

### VI.

Therefore to you the choirs of Heaven arise
    In reverence.   Key-stones are ye, every one,
    In God's sure house; fountains of benison,
Which Christ, the mighty Sea of love, supplies:
Visible angels lighting lower skies;
    How may we praise—how style you; call'd alone
    To sit in sackcloth on Christ's earthly throne,
Channels of living waters? golden ties
    From Christ's meek cradle to His throne on high?
    Bright shower-drops sparkling from God's orbed light?
    We hide our eyes, and ask what vesture bright
Shall clothe you, gather'd or from earth or sky,

[1 1 Pet. v. 5.]
[2 George Herbert, Rector of Bemerton, author of "The Temple,'
d. 1633.]
[3 Thomas à Kempis, author of "Imitatio Christi," d. 1471.]
4 See St John xx. 22, 23.

Ye chiefest servants of a suffering Lord,
The King of shame and sorrow ? what afford
Sky-tinctur'd grain to robe you ?   Other dress
Faith owns not, save her Master's lowliness.

## VII.

So not alone Christ's mission-crown on high
   Shall gird your brows with radiance, but the urn
   Of Heaven's own light in your true bosoms burn ;
For the great God Who fills eternity
Makes lowliest hearts His temple ; such we see,
   When to Faith's earliest morn our eyes we turn,
   And round th' all-conquering Cross of shame discern,
Kneeling in light, a suffering Hierarchy ;
   Thence, high and wide, 'mid Persecution's night,
   The East and West are with their glory bright ;
As on some festal eve in glorious Rome,
Far through the pillar'd shades of Peter's dome,
   A thousand glowing lamps fling light on high,
   Making their own calm day, their own pure sky
Around the holiest altar cross, whence springs
The mystic dove, shaking her golden wings.

## VIII.

" He that despiseth you doth Me despise."
   Lo ! at that call Faith her best robe prepares,
   And Heaven to Earth lets down the eternal stairs,
Through a long line of more than good or wise,
The high-born legates of the appeased skies
   Come down their avenue of sacred years ;
   Each in his hand Messiah's olive bears.
Ye priestly brotherhood, with reverent eyes
   Receive a guest from Heaven, your ancient seat
   Open ye, and Religion's deep retreat !
The dust of Time is on him, and Christ's mark,
Worldly reproach ; he bears the unquench'd spark
   To kindle into life earth's secret womb—
   To lighten or destroy, cheer or consume ;
Through chains, fire, sword, he bears thy last reprieve,
" He that receiveth you, doth Me receive ! "

# PART II.

# The Nave.

As for me, I will come into Thine house, even upon the multitude
of Thy mercy :

# The Porches.

## THE CHURCH IN HOPE.—THE CHURCH IN FEAR.

And in Thy fear will I worship toward Thy holy temple.

PSALM v. 7.

## The North Porch.

### *The Church in Hope.*

IT was the saddest time e'er lower'd on earth,
As Sin and Sorrow woke in Paradise,
When Mercy's voice 'mid frighted Nature's cries
    Broke forth, and pledg'd a Saviour's birth.[1]


When Noah saw how sternly Ruin gaunt
Sat on the grave of what did once rejoice,
'Twas then he saw the Bow, thrice heard the voice,
    " With thee shall stand My Covenant." [2]


Abram was going to the grave forlorn
And childless, whom the Lord took forth and shew'd
On night's dark vault a starry multitude,—
    Such, Abram, shall of thee be born.[3]


Exil'd, 'mid foes, and Egypt's withering shade,
Lean'd Israel on his staff beside his tomb,
'Twas light that broke from that dark gathering gloom,
    Which upon Judah's sceptre play'd.[4]


When Jesse's chosen son heav'd the deep sigh,
Forbidden with stain'd hands to build the shrine,
His harp reveal'd a holier Palestine,
    And spoke strange things of import high.[5]


The destin'd Assur came with armed stream,
And Judah heard the sound of Ephraim's chain,
And rent in thousand shivers on the plain
    Saw her long-promis'd Diadem.

[1 Gen. iii. 15.]      [2 *Ib.*, ix. 13.]      [3 *Ib.*, xv. 5.]
[4 *Ib.*, xlix. 10]      [5 1 Chron. xxviii. 5.]

And Chebar heard, and Ulai heard her cry ; [1]
'Twas that dark cloud which did on her alight,
Was loaded with glad Prophecy, and bright
    With the Eternal Saviour nigh.

Faith, listening to the lyre that spoke Him near,
Saw Lebanon's cedars wave to Seraph's hymn,
And 'mid the vale of Desolation dim
    A helm and moonlight-gleaming spear.

It was the guiltiest, darkest hour of man,
When the shock'd Earth shook in her agony,
And sun in shame had veil'd his sorrowing eye,
    'Twas then our better Birth began.

Yea, when sun, moon, and stars upon the skies
Shall shake, like figs upon the wither'd tree,
Then your redemption cometh speedily,
    And ye too may lift up your eyes.

Then, blessed Lord, when signs of coming ill
Shall speak Thy heavy vengeance at the door,
May we but cling unto Thy hand the more,
    And in a holier hope be still.

When doth the soul her higher wisdom see ?—
When Sorrow's clouds obscure her firmament,
'Tis then the many-colour'd bow is bent,
    To bid the birds of darkness flee.

Not when bright Summer winds her gladsome horn,
But when bluff Winter's blustering Charioteer
Chases the relics of the faded year,
    The lowly Child of Peace is born.

And in the gleams which thro' the darkness pour
Of Calvary, Poverty is our best wealth,
Sorrow our Comforter, and Sickness health,
    And Death of endless life the door.

[1 Ezekiel iii. 11-15 ; Dan. viii. 16.]

Yea, Sin herself, as by a charmed touch,
Hath unlearn'd her black nature, and brought down
High thoughts, a better righteousness to own,
    And, much forgiven, loveth much.

Thus have I seen at eve, when all the west
Marshall'd the shapes of darkness manifold,
A gleam hath turn'd to palaces of gold,
    From the bright sun gone to his rest.

# The Sepulchral Recesses.

## THE CHURCHMAN'S FRIENDS.

Yea, saith the Spirit, that they may rest from their labours : and their works do follow them.

REV. xiv. 13.

.

# 𝕿𝖍𝖊 𝕾𝖊𝖕𝖚𝖑𝖈𝖍𝖗𝖆𝖑 𝕽𝖊𝖈𝖊𝖘𝖘𝖊𝖘.

## *The Churchman's Friends.*

## LAUD.

[Archbishop of Canterbury ; martyred January 10, 1645. The poet specially dwells upon his zeal for the beauty of worship.]

THY spirit in thee strove
To cleanse and set in beauty free
The ancient shrines, mindful of Him Whose love
Swept with the scourge His Father's sanctuary.

Thy cloke was burning zeal,
Untaught the worldling's arts to wield,
But Innocence thy coat of triple steel,
And Loyalty and Truth thy sword and shield.

Thus arm'd against the tomb,
Thy dauntless course bore on to bind
Thy dying brows with deathless martyrdom,
Unsought by the true soul, but undeclin'd.

# KEN.

[The saintly Bishop of Bath and Wells ; deprived for refusing to swear allegiance to William III., 1689.   Died at Longleat, 1711.   After his deprivation, he largely employed himself in writing hymns.   The "sacred key" refers to his episcopal office, which he felt that the world could not interfere with.

The "Seven" who refused to read the Declaration of Indulgence at the bidding of King James, and were prosecuted by him and acquitted, were Sancroft, Archbishop of Canterbury, Lloyd, Ken, Turner, Lake, White, Trelawney, Bishops respectively of St Asaph, Bath and Wells, Ely, Chichester, Peterborough, and Bristol.

The "Five" who remained loyal to him after the Revolution were Sancroft, Turner, Ken, Frampton, and Lloyd.]

YE holy gates, open your calm repose,
Between him and the world your barriers close ;
Nought hath he but his lyre and sacred key,
Which the world gave not, nor can take away.
One of that Seven against a king he stood,
The world was with him in his fortitude.
One of that Five, he scorn'd her flattering breath,
And firm in strength which wisdom cherisheth,
Where Truth and Loyalty had mark'd the ground,
Stood by that suffering king, allegiance bound ;
Then as in him his Saviour stood reveal'd,
The world in anger rose, against him steel'd,
And drove him from her—Open your repose,
And, her and him between, your heavenly barriers close.

## KING CHARLES I.

[Martyred January 30, 1649.]

I SAW a Royal Form with eye upturn'd,
  Rising from furnace of affliction free,
  And knew that brow of deep serenity,
Whereon, methought, a crown of glory burn'd,
With a calm smile, as if the death-cry turn'd
  On his freed ear to seraph sounds on high!
  Still in the guilty place the hideous cry
Bark'd impotent.   In quiet hope inurn'd
Was his poor fleshly mantle, but the breath
  Of our bad world o'er this unquiet stage
Flouts his blest name, unpardon'd e'en in death.
And thus his holy shade on earth beneath,
  Still walks 'mid evil tongues from age to age
  Bearing the cross, his Master's heritage.
But no unkindly word for evermore
Can reach his rest, or pass th' eternal door.

### KETTLEWELL.

[Vicar of Coleshill; deprived as non-juror in 1688. Died 1695. His "Christian Obedience" is a very noble book. His friend Robert Nelson said of him, that his governing principles were Humility, Sincerity, Meekness, and Universal Charity.]

Is there a form in England's Church enshrin'd,
   Which some bright guardian Angel doth invest
   With his own hues, in which her mien imprest,
And her transforming spirit throughly shin'd,
In calm obedience lovingly resign'd?
   'Tis Coleshill's saint, in meekness manifest,—
   He whom in trial's hour she sweetly blest
With patient wisdom, and so disciplin'd
   To keep his garments, that for him she won
   From th' Eucharistic fount of Benison
Stern reverential Truth; then Charity
   Made his meek heart an altar, and thereon
Burn'd like some fragrant incense, to the sky
In holy prayers rising continually.

## TAYLOR.

[Bishop of Down and Connor, d. 1667 ; called the English Chrysostom
for the beauty of his eloquence.   The poet alludes to his best-known
work, " Holy Living and Dying," and also to his " Golden Grove," a
devotional work.   He was fined heavily and imprisoned for attaching
himself to Charles I.

LIKE a woof where jewels gleam,
 Where the rubies beam,
Where the colours of all skies,
 And "the beryl lies,"[1]
Such is thy unfetter'd line,
 Saint and sage benign.

Thou shalt teach us from on high
 How to live and die.
How the golden hues of love
 Tinge the fading grove,
Dressing Autumn's drear decay
 With the gleams of day.

Thou the channels of Heaven's grace
 Thro' all time shalt trace,
And thine untun'd eloquence
 Its deep stores dispense,
In thy soul laid manifold
 On the floor untold.

Early seen at Heaven's high door
 Thy full soul to pour,
If of Angel's minstrelsy
 Aught should wander nigh,
Watching for a sweeter strain
 Wilder'd man to gain.

Prison'd friend of martyr king,
 Never flagg'd thy wing.
Upward still thy spirit draws
 In life-giving laws,
Training with stern discipline
 To the towers divine.

[1] See his Hymn on Heaven.

Come, my people, enter thou into thy chambers, and shut thy doors about thee : hide thyself as it were for a little moment, until the indignation be overpast.

ISAIAH xxvi. 20.

# The Oratories.

## CONSOLATIONS AND STRONGHOLDS.

When thou prayest, enter into thy closet, and when thou hast shut thy door, pray to thy Father which is in secret : and thy Father which seeth in secret shall reward thee openly.

ST MATTHEW vi. 6.

## The Oratories.

*Consolations and Strongholds.*

---

### DISTANT CHURCH MUSIC.

My spirit hath gone up in yonder cloud
Of solemn and sweet sound—the many-voic'd
   Peal upon peal, and now
   The choral voice alone

At door of Heaven.   My soul is all unsphered,
Soaring and soaring on the crystal car
   Of airy sweetness borne,
   And drinks ethereal air

Amid celestial shapes.   I hear a voice
Alone before the Trinal Majesty,
   Singing the Eternal Lamb,
   While Silence sits aloof.

Twilight of unimagin'd Deity
It seems, save where, like thousand setting suns,
   Heaven's portal darkly gleams,—
   He hath gone down to man.

Far hath He thrown His crown to stars of Heaven,
And to the skies His clear empyreal robe,
   To lightning His bright spear,
   And to the clouds His bow.[1]

A crown awaits Thee there, but not of gold,—
And who is she Thy coming harbingers?
   No starry watchmen near
   Creation's cradle set,

No kingly pursuivants.   But sackcloth-rob'd
Heard stilly 'tween the torrent's fitful sound,

[1] The idea is from Herbert, and carried on in the last stanza.

And wild-bird's cry forlorn,
'Mid rocks, and desert caves

Repentance' voice !—Who on Thy goings wait?
No sun-bright legionry, but Sorrow meek,
   Pity, meek Sorrow's child,
   And Peace, of Pardon born.

While Hope prepares her gleaming car; from high
With arms outstretch'd, out of a golden cloud
   Righteousness leaning down
   Hath kissed exil'd Peace.

To gates of darkness hies black-hooded Night,  ·
And on her waning brow lingers the Moon,
   With silver bow to greet
   Uprising glory's Sun.

E'en now upon th' horizon Morning walks
Doffing to Night her mantle grey, and stands
   In gold and gleaming vest,
   And glittering shafts reveal'd.

Ye waiting at th' eternal gate, with robes
Of penitential Sorrow, wash'd in blood,
   And odorous lamps well trimm'd,
   Your long-lov'd Lord to greet,

Lift up your eyes !  E'en now His coming glows
Where, on the skirt of yon Heaven-kissing hill,
   The trees stand motionless
   Upon the silvery dawn.

Deep Ocean treasures all her gems unseen,
To pave an archway to the eternal door,
   And Earth doth rear her flowers
   To strew your heavenly road.

The Stars on high shall be your diadem,
The Skies shall lend their rays to weave your robes,
   And Iris stain the woof,
   · Sons of th' eternal morn.

## THE DOXOLOGY.

### I.

THE threefold heavens, of glorious height,
Are made One dwelling for Thy might,
Set upon pillars of the light.

The earth, and sea, and blue-arch'd air,
Do form below One temple fair,
Thy footstool 'neath the heavenly stair.

Sun, Moon, and Stars, in Heaven's great deep
Their living watch obedient keep,
Moving as One, and never sleep.

### II.

Angels and men and brutes beneath
Make up Creation's triple wreath,
Which only liveth in Thy breath.

In fish and birds and beasts around,
One wondrous character is found,
The skirt which doth Thy mantle bound.

And Nature's three fair realms convey
One note through this our earthly day,
Dying in distance far away.

### III.

With Three arch'd roofs Thy temple springs,
Where music spreads melodious wings,
And all around One glory brings.

And Future, Past, and Present Time,
Together build One shrine sublime,
That doth prolong the ample chime.

While spirit, soul, and clay-born seat,
Warm'd by the living Paraclete,
Shall be Thy threefold mansion meet.

## THE ATHANASIAN CREED.

O WARNING voice, from Truth's eternal shrine
　　Proceeding, where the great Archangel sings,
Through threefold arching piles, on sounds divine,

　　And the live thunder of melodious wings
Rising in adoration !　Mother dear,
　　To thy mysterious breast my spirit clings

Then most, when that appalling voice I hear :--
　　There at the sound of those thy stern alarms
I hide, and on the world look back and fear ;

　　For she would tempt me from thy sheltering arms,
And stop thy voice, which baffled Pride disdains,
　　And the dread sound of never-dying harms.

Vain thought ! th' o'erwhelming Future yet remains,
　　Though Ebal and Gerizim's voice be still,
The everlasting Now and penal chains.

　　And from Thine accents hide us as we will,
Death draws aside the screen.　Then wherefore flee
　　With birds of darkness to the caves of ill ?

Rather in garb of our deep poverty
　　Let us stand forth before Thee, not to gaze,
But tremble, with the heart's adoring knee,

　　Full in the light of Thy meridian blaze.
Nor leave Thou us in the dark mysteries
　　Of our bad hearts to wander, and in ways

Of our own darkness, lest we, seeming wise,
　　Shrine Thee in shape of some foul deity,
And in our unbaptized phantasies

　　Think wickedly that God is such as we,—
Some Jove, or Pan, or Ashtaroth unclean,—
　　So may we 'scape Thy judgment.—Dread the sea

Of glory which enshrouds Thee, yet unseen,
   And in the path whereon Thy light doth burn,
Ere that we pass th' inevitable screen,

   Well need we walk and fear : to Thee we turn
For help, nor on Thy glory gaze too bold.
   O sternly kind, and kindest when most stern,

Ancient of Mothers, in thy barriers old
   With them that love thee is best liberty !
Fain would we hide us in thy sheltering fold.

   By thee baptiz'd into the Eternal Three,
Blest Arbitress of holiest discipline,
   In the world's freedom let me not be free,

But follow mine own will in following thine.
   To Christ our Rock with dripping weeds we cling,
While Ocean roars beneath ; fled to thy shrine

   May Heaven's own Dove, on Contemplation's wing,
Be o'er us, nurturing each holier choice,
   And all around thy calmer influence bring.

Then let me ever hear thy awful voice,
   Deep warning, deep adoring : while we sing
We tremble, but in trembling we rejoice.


### FAST DAYS.

WHILE to the tomb we tread this pilgrimage,
   Sorrow will wait upon us, and be ours
E'en as our shadow, where on Life's dim stage
   Falls the celestial light from Eden's bowers.

Then it were wise to win her for our friend,
   Who must be our companion, so to gain
That she may help us to our journey's end,
   So may we love her yoke, nor feel the chain.

Lest we should exile take for home of ease,
   Shadows for truth, for shore the billow's breast,
Our trial for acceptance and release,
   The vale of tears for mountain of our rest.


Such Sorrow is sent down by pitying Heaven,
   The mantle which from Jesus fell below,
To His own chosen in His mercy given,
   The last best boon He could on earth bestow.


Nor wonder that the widow'd Church should sound
   Of sadness : those are mourners Christ hath blest,
Who watch with her their annual, weekly round,
   And in obedience find the promis'd rest.


A shelter from ourselves her sacred call,
   Lest the self-humbling soul might haply make
Her penance glory—lest her mourner's pall
   Self-form'd, for trappings of her pride she take.


Nor deem such penance hard, nor fondly dream
   Of Herod's ease in the imperial hall,
But seek the Baptist by the desert stream,
   And thou shalt see the light on Jesus fall :


Yea haply so be brought with Christ to pray
   In His own secret mount—or in His word
Where Moses and Elias witness pay,
   To watch, till Heaven-reveal'd ye see the Lord.


Nor deem such penance hard—thence from the soul
   The cords of flesh are loos'd, and earthly woes
Lose half their power to harm, while self-control
   Learns that blest freedom which she only knows.


Thence is our hope to manlier aims subdued,
   And purg'd from earthly mists the mental eye,
To gird herself with growing fortitude,
   To see the gates of immortality,

Beyond the vale of woes ; while far between,
   In watchings and in fastings train'd of yore,
Martyrs and Saints, in glorious order seen,
   Follow the Man of Sorrows gone before.

Now sphered in orbs of light to us they call :
   The eve precedes with penitential woes,
And ushers in the holier festival,
   The shadow which their glory earthward throws.

Many the gates of Hell, and every gate
   Is but each vice which man's dark temper sways,
And Christ alone can raise our fallen state,
   In fasting found, and prayer, and watchful ways.

They stayed up his hands, the one on the one side, and the other
on the other side, until the going down of the sun.

EXODUS xvii. 12.

# The Transepts.

## THE PSALMS.

## THE EPISTLE AND GOSPEL.

All the day long I have stretched forth my hands unto a disobedient
and gainsaying people.

ROMANS x. 21.

## The North Transept.

### THE PSALMS.

*(Jesus Christ in Prophecy.)*

#### I.

Not to those heights where holy Herbert sits,
 Or Heaven-taught Ken awakes the sounding wire,
Nor where beyond the shade of Ambrose flits
 O'er sacred streams, or leaning o'er the lyre
 Peace-loving Nazianzen [1] leads the quire,—
Not to those haunts where saintly men have trod,
 And hung their harps, but further yet and higher,
Where Siloa's stream, woke by th' unearthly rod,
Springs forth a fountain pure beneath the mount of God.[2]

#### II.

Yea, and the Church shall love that hallowed fount,
 Rivers of God, blest scenes, the secret height
Where David sat, his Sion's holy mount,
 More than all-glowing strains of human spright;[3]
 For Heaven-born Truth shrinks from sublunar light,
And rather wears the veil of David's hymn
 Than the full glare of day, and oft from sight,
In parable and type and shadows dim,
There hides her holier face and wings of Seraphim.[4]

[1] The four holy men here named were all famous poetical writers. Some of the hymns of St Ambrose are used in our public worship.]
 [2] Milton's "Paradise Lost." I. 11.]
 [3] Spright=cheerful spirit.]
 [4] It is curious to note that our author expresses the preference of the Church for the Psalms rather than for Hymns directly expressing Christian doctrine. At the time when this was written Hymns were exclusively used in churches where the distinctive doctrine was of the so-called "Evangelical" type, and opposed to that taught by the author.]

### III.

By figure, rite, and storied mysteries,
    The glorious light, in highest Heaven that dwells,
Tempers its image to man's feebler eyes,
    Softly reflected in terrestrial wells.
While to each rising thought true Wisdom tells
Of purer heights—whate'er of good desire,
    Of love, or thought serene the bosom swells,
There they on bodiless wings to Heaven aspire,
And gain, perchance, a gleam of that diviner fire.

### IV.

While Hope with Sorrow mingles, as if still
    We walk'd in Eden, and felt God was nigh ;
Or 'neath the shade of some o'erhanging hill
    An Angel guest attun'd his melody
    To better things, which hidden are on high,
Blending therein Mortality's poor tale
    Of sad offendings ; while we listening by
Discern his lineaments, all silvery pale,
Lightening the mists that move in Death's dim-peopled vale.

### V.

O griefs of fall'n mankind and sympathies
    Of Heaven, like quiet stars that on the night
Look forth, and tell of their own happier skies.
    There Christ Himself conceals from ruder sight
    Himself, and His own sorrows infinite,
Beneath the robe of fleshly types, which hide
    His glory, dimly seen in skirts of light,—
Himself, and in Himself His suffering Bride,
Present to strengthen her, ta'en from His bleeding side.

## VI.

As when the Moon, hid in some woodland maze,
    Lights all with her own meek magnificence,
And oft displays her shadows—the rapt gaze,
    Kindling at her retiring more intense,[1]
    Labours to view her ; she from her dim fence
Oft opens on the glade no more conceal'd ;
    Thus thro' the lore, lit by His influence,
The Christian's Lord oft stands, to sight reveal'd,
And shews, in clearer heights, His all-protecting shield.

## VII.

From everlasting are His goings, this
    Is the deep note, wherewith his widow'd Dove
Pleads, and her note of Sorrow blends with His.
    Here, 'mid the unfailing citadels above,
    His children walk with Him ; here with Him prove
Pilgrims on earth below, from age to age ;
    Here, link'd in suffering, may they learn His love,
And hide their joys and sorrows in the page,
Wherein with Him He blends His ransom'd heritage.

## VIII.

Ye holy strains, on David's harp that hung,
    Tabor and little Hermon to your call,
And Jordan's willowy banks responsive sung :
    Ye with soft wings, like Angel friends, when all
    Seem'd to forsake, have sooth'd the Martyr's thrall ;
Some high-soul'd Laud, in suffering fortitude ;
    Some captive Taylor by his prison wall ;
And one by Cherwell's banks, in happier mood,
Hath woo'd your choral voice to soothe his solitude.[2]

[1] Adjective used for adverb.]
[2] Bishop Horne. [See his Life by Jones of Nayland, p. 111.]

## IX.

Nor learned cell alone, nor sacred pile—
   Made animate with sweetness, flowing o'er
The music-rolling roof, and branching aisle—
   But widow'd Eld, that, in some cottage poor,
   Sitteth alone by the eternal shore,
With your deep inspirations hath been young;
   Your beauteous torch hath lit Death's shadowy door,
And strengthen'd by your staff, and cheering tongue,
The failing spirit walks unfading groves among.

## X.

Oh, my sad soul is weary with Earth's wrong—
   Evil of men, and worldly vanity;—
Give me the music of your heavenly song,—
   Sion, nurse of our hopes, for thee I sigh;—
   Give me the music of your minstrelsy,
Which hath its echo in the heart alone!
   Oh, waken up that Angel company,
That sleeps in your deep chords—from your pure throne
Come forth, lift my weak soul to your untroubled zone;

## XI.

Come to me, Angel guests! whatever springs
   In me of passion, or of earthly pride,
Shall flee at sound of your celestial wings;
   O gentle Psalmist, other thoughts abide
   With thee, how have I scared thee? to my side
Come again, tranquil spirit; oh, unrol
   Thy sweet melodious fulness o'er the tide
Of my wild tossing thoughts, touch my sad soul,
And let me own again thy mastering soft control!

## XII.

Spirit of prayer and praise, with gentle hand
　　Thou lead'st me, calming every wayward mood,
Thro' storied scenes and haunts of sacred land,
　　Unto a dim and shadowy solitude,
　　Where One is in a garden dropping blood.
Lo, here comes one with accents of a friend ;[1]
　　Gethsemane, is this thy night so rude?
On yon dark mound the cup of woe they blend ;[2]
There 'neath mysterious shades they for thy robe contend.[3]


## XIII.

How shall we learn in this our fleeting breath
　　The scale and measure of mortality,
Save communing with Thy life-giving death,
　　With stern bereavement's haggard family
　　Thy sole attendants ?　How else learn to die,
Or how to live?　How else our strength discern,
　　Our true desert, our price, our misery,
Our happiness—how else our Maker learn,
The depth, the breadth, the height of Mercy's bounteous
　　urn ?


## XIV.

And where shall we behold th' Eternal Son,
　　Save in these strains, wherein the car of Love
In greatness of its strength is travelling on,
　　Through Time's dark shadows which around her move?
　　Her silver wings here plumes the earth-soil'd Dove,
And feels again life's sunshine gleaming warm ;
　　Here Hope, Devotion's handmaid, fain would prove
The covenant bow encircling her bright form,
And lets her radiant vest flow o'er the cloud and storm.

---

[1] Ps. xli. 9.　　[2] Ps. lxix. 22.　　[3] Ps. xxii. 18.

## XV.

'Tis thus Imagination's airy swell
    Bears on the soul, and fills her buoyant wing ;
Oft has she come with foulest airs from Hell ;
    Here purer gales their sweet compulsion bring
    From the fresh haunts of never-fading spring ;
Sure thus to school our fancies it were wise,
    That they may wait on our eternal King,
Gathering meek thoughts upon His praise to rise,
Else vanities they wed, and lurk in earthly guise.

## XVI.

Ever, sweet Psalmist, lead the sounding key,
    Humbling to duteous calm the thoughts that move
Responsive to our sacred Liturgy,
    That they on holier wings may soar above
    To Mercy's seat.   O Bard of Heaven-taught love,
Striving in vain thy wounded heart to hide,
    Soul-stricken mourner, like the bleeding dove
Deeper and deeper clasping 'neath her side
The barbs that drink her life, and in her heart abide.

## XVII.

Still let me cull thy flowers of Paradise,
    Sweet flowers, that ever bloom on Sorrow's brink,
Water'd with penitence and holy sighs ;
    And when within me my weak soul doth sink,
    Oft at thy living fountains let me drink,
Springs which no wintry fetters can repress,
    Nor sun, nor scorching whirlwind, cause to shrink.—
I hew'd me wells in the world's wilderness,
Wearied and worn I sought, and found but bitterness.

## XVIII.

I sought and found but bitterness—and now,
   Blest Tree of Calvary, do thou abide
In the deep fount whence our affections flow,
   Which else were Marah.[1]  How hast thou supplied
   Light 'mid my wanderings, and at my side
Rais'd dearest friends, pitying my lost estate,
   In whom I something of Thy light descried,
And learn'd of them my former self to hate,
Led onward by the hand toward the heavenly gate !

## XIX.

These are but ministers of Thy sure love,
   By which Thou gently to Thyself wouldst lead,
And now what would I seek, but Thee above?
   Our goodliest friends on earth from Thee proceed,
   And unto Thee return ; but our deep need
Thou only in Thy fulness canst sustain :
   Upon Thine earthly plenteousness we feed,
But yet the choicest gifts of Earth disdain,
And feel in every nook around our house of pain,

## XX.

And find Thee not.  Then in that sacred chord
   We hear from unseen heights a glorious song,
Of panoplies divine and shield and sword,—
   Faith in unearthly armour bold and strong,
   And strains which to Thy ransom'd host belong.
Then, where from high the showering sunbeams fall
   Amid th' encircling mists of grief and wrong,
Is seen to rise th' Eternal City's wall,
While Earth responds to Heaven, and deep to deep doth call.

## XXI.

For Truth beside that crystal sea doth stand,  .
   Spher'd in her own bright radiance, like a shrine,
And holds a mystic lamp in her right-hand,

---

[1] Exodus xv. 23.

Fill'd with the light of Poesy divine ;
    And wheresoe'er she doth that light incline,
Something celestial shines on us awhile,
    And we with yearnings of lost Eden pine ;
Man's heart its fulness labouring to beguile,
Unburden'd of itself doth to her music smile.


## XXII.

Thus when with man's deep soul God's Spirit wrought,
    They spoke of things more glorious than they knew,
Blending prophetic dreams with mortal thought.
    Then fabling bards the shadows of the true
    From other wells of inspiration drew ;
The great dissembler came with wings of light,
    O'er meaner things th' enchanter's mantle threw,
Kindling to burning thoughts th' enraptur'd sprite,
Like meteors that would vie with living stars of light.


## XXIII.

Then the old world with fabled heroes rung,
    Men like to gods, and gods more frail than they ;
O'er his lone harp the great Pelides[1] hung,
    Sitting by Ocean's solitary spray ;
    And the fam'd Bard from Chios bent his way ;[2]
Of mighty wars the marvellous minstrel told,
    Earth and Heaven leagu'd in battailous affray,
Prowess in arms and high achievements bold,
And that his homeless chief in wanderings grown old.

[1 " Pelides "—Achilles. " Iliad," ix. 186 ff.—Thus translated by
Lord Derby :—
        " When to the ships they came, where lay
        The warlike Myrmidons, their chief they found,
        His spirit soothing with a sweet-toned lyre
        Of curious work with silver-band adorned.
        .   .   .   .   .   On this he played
        Soothing his soul, and sang of warriors' deeds."]
    [2] Homer.

## XXIV.

But one there was who sat by Siloa's stream
  And converse held with God ; a poet's tear
He shed, but not of hate or love the theme.
  He too had borne the helmet and the spear,
  And now the crown of Eastern Kings did wear ;
With nobler thoughts his strains arise and cease,
  With one Whose presence to his soul was dear,
His strains they were of holiness and peace,
And One that should arise Creation to release.


## XXV.

He sang of the commandments wise and true,
  Which hold the Heavens and Earth in golden chain,
And man's delinquency to vengeance due,
  That golden chain all powerless to retain,
  By which he might those blissful seats regain.
He sang of things before his spirit brought,
  Visions of God, and mansions far from pain :
Nor fathom'd half his labouring fancy wrought,
Lost in the Infinite of his own holier thought.


## XXVI.

He sang of the commandments true and just,
  Of Him Who rolling stars holds in His hand,
And hearts of men who in His guidance trust ;
  He call'd on earth and Heaven, on sea and land,
  With Him before th' Eternal throne to stand,
On trees, and brutes, and stars before His throne
  To stand, united in fraternal band,
The glories of their common Lord to own,
And sing their great Creator, Three in One.

## XXVII.

He sang of the commandments just and good,
    Sole rest of man below and joy above :
And oft his earthly weeds at Siloa's flood,
    Rent by turmoils with which his spirit strove,
    He wash'd in streams of all-pervading Love,
And put on garments of celestial Praise.
    Then was God's Presence seen in all that move,
As when the sun, all arm'd with glittering rays,
Comes forth from night's dark tent, and o'er Heaven's arch
    way strays.

## XXVIII.

He sang of the commandments good and great,
    Without which, mirror'd in the heavenly glass,
There were no concord in angelic state,
    Nor harmonies on high.    All earth as grass
    Shall fade away, the skies to nothing pass,
Born of the Breath of the life-giving Word
    These living laws shall, from the dying mass,
Lead to the presence of th' Eternal Lord,
And better strength to run His high behests afford.

## XXIX.

Ye laws that walk in starry mansions, sweet
    As melodies of mountain pipe, which fill
The frame responsive and obedient feet,
    So would I listen to your sounds, until
    Ye might to action stir my sluggard will ;
I would be deaf to all but your deep tongue,
    And run your heavenly ways : by your dread thrill
May I to duteous discipline be strong,
Till in your freshening bloom I grow for ever young.

In the midst of the street, and on either side of the river, was there
the Tree of Life—

**North Aisle.**      **Middle Aisle.**      **South Aisle.**

**The Lord's Prayer.**      **Holy Scripture.**      **The Creed.**

And the leaves of the Tree were for the healing of the nations.

REV. xxii. 2.

D

## The North Aisle.

### The Lord's Prayer.

I. *Varieties in Nature combined with identity.* II. *The same to be observed in the Lord's Prayer.* III. *A Paraphrase of it in the Baptismal Service.* IV. *In the Daily Prayers.* V. *In the Litany.* VI. *In the Ante-Communion.* VII. *In the Post-Communion Service.* VIII. *In the Marriage Service.* IX. *In the Burial Service.* X. *Its sacredness and mysterious depth.* XI. *Its divine origin, and the future hopes contained therein.* XII. *Its effect in private devotion in the different ages of life.* XIII. *The Conclusion.*

----

Oh, that I knew how all thy lights combine,
And the configurations of their glory !
     \*       \*      \*       \*

Such are thy secrets ; which my life makes good,
And comments on thee.   For in every thing
Thy words do find me out.

*Herbert.*

### I.

THE Moon upon her silver height
Seems varying with the varying night;
Still varying seems, though still the same
Since out of Evening's door she came ;
To lead some traveller journeying on,
Her cheering mantle o'er him thrown.
First issues forth with burnish'd crest
Looking upon the golden west,—
A knight in virgin armour drest,
Pledging herself companion sure
Thro' hours of darkness to endure:
Then seems descended from her tower
To kindle up some wintry bower :
And turns the leafless branches bright
Into an hermitage of light,
Or temple strange of living gold
With Gothic traceries manifold.
Then silently breaks forth to view,
Walking along the sea of blue ;

Anon with rising clouds contending,
And with their gloom her glory blending ;
They gather 'neath her steps of brightness,
A pedestal of glowing whiteness.
Thus leads thro' night, then melts away
Into the sunshine of the day.
With brow unchang'd the while she dwells,
In Heaven's serener citadels,
But seems with us as here we range
To thread the path of interchange.

Who live beside the solemn Sea,
And love his simple majesty,
Still ever new, in alter'd mien
His untransformed shape have seen.
Now as they sit his margin nigh,
He lifts his hands and voice on high,
No thought can trace his hidden treasure,
His beauty, strength, or vastness measure.
Now while they other scenes pursue,
The hills between, in arching blue,
He gathers in his silver length
All darkly to a bow of strength.—
Now man's meek friend, upon his breast
He bears him hous'd in sea-born nest.—
Now God's unsullied temple fair,
For man hath left no traces there.—
Now aye unchang'd, yet ever changing,
To caves unfathom'd boundless ranging ;
Now seems to lay his vastness by
To minister to thought and eye.

A faithful Friend, best boon of Heaven
Unto some favour'd mortal given,
Tho' still the same, yet varying still,
Our each successive want to fill,
Beneath life's ever fitful hue
To us he bears an aspect new.
Round childhood's path a happy charm,
In age a tried supporting arm ;
A chastening drop in cup of gladness,
A light to paint the mists of sadness :
To cheer, to.chide, to teach, to learn,
Sad or severe, serene or stern.

Whatever form his presence wears
That presence every form endears.
Till Faith descries in that dear love
The messenger from One above,
Faint emblem of a better Friend,
Who walks with us till life shall end.


## II.

E'en such in its simplicity
Containing things for man too high,
The holy Prayer which Jesus taught !
A well too deep for mortal thought,
But where his want may ever turn,
And draw with ever-welcome urn.
On childhood's dawn it doth unfold
Its treasures, and when life is old
Unfolding still yet all untold.
Ever transform'd to meet our needs,
Oft as Devotion counts her beads,
As if those beads had caught the light,
In her celestial girdle bright,
But each with its own colours dight.
Thus whensoe'er that Prayer is heard,
Fresh thoughts are in each solemn word ;
An orb of light, come from the skies,
To kindle holy Liturgies ;
It gathers and gives back their rays,
Now turn'd to prayer, and now to praise.
    Thus is Thy word, unearthly wise,
A fire that lights each sacrifice ;
'Tis that, which in Thine earthly shrine,
Clothes our desires with form divine.
To enter so more worthily
The place of Thy dread Majesty.
Upon that incense doth arise
A holy Angel to the skies,
And there all cloth'd with other wings,
'Neath th' Intercessor's feet it springs.
Yea, could we see within that cloud
Of incense, from its earthly shroud

Its glorious fulness evermore
Unfolding to the heavenly door,
We there, reveal'd to mortal eye,
Should Angels, on glad ministry
Ascending and descending see.


## III.

*In the Baptismal Service.*

First on Baptismal waters bright
It seems to move, a face of light,
And when around we kneel and pray,
The holy accents seem to say,;

" Our Father, freed from error's chain
　　May we thy children be,
At this blest Fountain born again
　　To filial liberty.

All things are changing, Thou the same,
　　Thou art our heavenly home ;
Be hallowed here our Father's Name,
　　Until His kingdom come.

Lo, to Thy kingdom here below
　　We little children bring,
For to that kingdom such we know
　　The meetest offering.

That they in Thee may here put on
　　Thy kingdom's panoply ;
And in the path of duty run,
　　Like children of the sky.

Oft as breaks out their mother's stain,
　　While they advance to Heaven,
Children in love may they remain,
　　Forgiving and forgiv'n.

Let nought allure them from Thy word,
   Or tempt their spirits frail,
But should they fall, yet, blessed Lord,
   Let evil not prevail."

But when our Childhood's morn was ending,
And we 'neath holy hands were bending,[1]
Beside that altar's witness-stone
That prayer had caught an altered tone.
The cheek with shame and hope was burning,
To a lost Father's house returning ;
It seem'd to chide, and yet to cheer,
And to that blending hope and fear
It brought our endless birthright near,
And from the rude world seem'd to sever,
Binding us to that shrine for ever.


## IV.

### *In the Daily Service.*

At morn or eve when worldly Care
Would seek to breathe the calmer air
Of Thy pure temple ; Peace is there,
But not for her.  At mercy gate
Repentance stands, made wise too late,
Half lifts the latch, as one in guise
To enter, but with tearful eyes
Sees her lost heritage, and sighs.[2]
But watching for returning grief,
The great Absolver with relief
Stands by the door, and bears the key
O'er Penitence on bended knee :[3]
Then blending accents, sweet to save,
Come like the gale on sullen wave,
When Day is at his western cave.

" Our Father, Who dost dwell above,
   May we find rest in Thy dear love,
   And sanctify in heart Thy Name :

---

[1] At Confirmation.    [2] The Confession.    [3] The Absolution.

Where else shall sinner hide his shame,
When rising and departing Sun
But numbers duties left undone,
And nearer brings th' Eternal throne !

May we, advancing that to meet,
Feel daily more beneath our feet
The better strength which doth the will,
And seeth Thee, and so is still :
And borne on Thy sustaining arm,
Which daily feeds, and keeps from harm,
The wrath of man by love disarm.
The sole assurance that we live,
Is that we others thus forgive,
And day and night, where shall we flee
The wily Tempter, but to Thee ?
Dim shadows range this earthly cell,
The Kingdom and the Glory dwell
With Thee, alone unchangeable."

## V.

### *In the Litany.*

Who long in light of prayer abide,
As in the Sun's bright gushing tide,
Find hidden stains break forth within,
Like spots upon the leopard's skin.
Now spreading thro' the ample shrine,
Prayer sounds the seas of Love divine,
And now the deeps of crime and woe
Thro' changeful scenes of Life below.
Now Fear doth wake and onward press,
Girding her loins with lowliness,
Till seeing Thee she sinks from high,
In thoughts of her deep poverty ;
And with poor Bartimæus blind
Seeks in the dark Thy presence kind ;[1]
Now with Thine accents, deep and clear,
She holds Thy mantle in calm fear.

[1] The Sentences before the Lord's Prayer in the Litany.

" Like as a Father his own children loves,
　So unto those that fear Thee Thou art kind,
　　　For Thine own glorious name,
　　　Turn from us our deserts !

So may Thy Kingdom come, on whose blest shore
These hosts of woe and crime shall war no more,
　　　But East and West be set
　　　Our sins and us between.

Strengthen and comfort, raise us and support,
So may Thy will be done, as 'tis in Heaven :
　　　And dews of blessing fall
　　　On the fruit-bearing earth !

By all Thy works that we might be forgiven,
Thy Love, Thy Prayer, Thy Baptism, and Thy Grave,
　　　From envy and from hate,
　　　Deliver us, Good Lord.

Deliver us from the dark Tempter's wiles,
In Sorrow's hour and in the hour of wealth,
　　　So 'neath our feet at last
　　　The Serpent may be laid."

　　'Tis thus, by all Thy mercies old,
　　By all our fathers have us told,
　　Thus by Thy Love are we made bold.


## VI.

### *In the Ante-Communion.*

But when, the white-robed Altar nigh,
The chain was let down from on high,
Which from His Cross unto His throne
Doth bind His children all in one,
As heavy-laden souls draw near
To hear dread Sinai's voice of fear,
Responsively to our deep wound,
That Prayer assumes another sound.

" Out of a world of grief and wrong,
　Where we have wandered all too long,
　To Thee our Father we return,
　　Do Thou not spurn !

Thou art in Heaven and we on earth,
Then weigh us not by our own worth,
May we henceforth in reverent awe
　　So keep Thy law,

That we may hallow Thy Great Name !
Lay on our lips Thine altar flame,
And that from Thee no more we roam,
　　Thy Kingdom come.

For only they, who do Thy will,
Shall Thine Eternal Kingdom fill,
Then may we throughout this our night
　　Walk in Thy Light !

Thou art our Father, only Good,
Wilt Thou not give us that blest food ?
We on Thine altar for Thine aid
　　Ourselves have laid,

Unworthy—yet in deed or thought,
If our own brother hath done aught,
As we on Thy forgiveness live,
　　So we forgive.

Around us are the shafts of ill,
O hide us in Thy holy hill,
That we in th' evil day may stand,
　　Holding Thy hand ! "

The cloud hath past, which hung thereon,
And Moses and Elias gone,[1]
And Thou art standing by alone.

---

[1] Alluding to the Scriptures, *i.e.*, the Law and the Prophets, which have been read before the Communion.

## VII.

*In the Post-Communion.*

And now the fount of Love o'erflows,
And the worn spirit finds repose ;
Lord, at Thy feet, in thrilling fear,
Lifts up her eye, and wipes the tear,
And with Thy Prayer again draws near.

" Our Father, knit in Thy dear Son,
    In celestial union,
Thy Name we hallow, and adore,
    Praising Thee for evermore.
And hasten till Thy kingdom come,
    Which is our eternal home.
May we till that blest palm be won,
    On the path of duty run.
With Angels and Archangels high,
    And the heavenly company,
inging of Thine immortal love,
    As Thine Angels sing above.

O daily from th' angelic hall,
    This life-giving food let fall,
And knit us in the holy tie ·
    Of ne'er-failing charity.
That from Thine own parental sway,
    Nought may lead our feet astray,
Ever attun'd in heart to sing
    Thee our everlasting King,
Whose Glory is our home on high,
    And His name best Panoply."

Thus when Thy love hath made us strong,
That Prayer becomes the pilgrim's song.

## VIII.

*In the Marriage Service.*

But lo, a small and silent train
Is gather'd 'neath the pictur'd pane,
Where ancient Saints in light profound,

Stand, like stern witnesses, around ;
Whose rainbow hues now play below
Fitfully on the vest of snow : [1]
'Tis bridal Love that doth repair
To light her holy torch-light there.
Varied as Morning's eastern door,
That Prayer hath other thoughts in store :
As on some Dove's soft mantling breast
When vernal lights or shadows rest,
There come forth interchangeably
An emerald, gold, or silver dye,
Which 'neath the secret colour lie.

" O Thou, of Whom all families
  In Earth and Heaven are named, may that Name,
Which all our wills and wishes sanctifies,

  Be hallowed in each household ; may the flame
From off Thine Altar light the peaceful hearth,
  And patriarchal blessings crown the same !

A type of Thy true kingdom here on earth,
  An household, over which Thy holy Dove
Broods, nurturing below to Heaven-taught worth,

  Angelic order, and harmonious love.
The ministering elements in Thy hand lie,
  Open for them Thy storehouses above :—-

Their spirits clothe with the meek poverty
  Of the true Bridegroom, His law to fulfil,
In mutual forbearing charity.

  Stand Thou about them night and day, that ill
May not approach their dwelling, nor sin's bane
  Tempt forth, then blast with death the wandering will.

So rise they on that bridal morn again,
  When all as Angels [2] Thy great Kingdom fill,
And in Thine everlasting glory reign ! "

[1] The effect of light falling through the painted windows.
[2] " They neither marry nor are given in marriage, but are as the
Angels."—St Mark xii. 25.

## IX.

*In the Burial Service.*

But lo, where by yon gleaming tower
The Sun sinks to his western bower,
As weeping mourners stand around,
Like Evening dews there falls a sound
On hearts by sorrow withered,—
The words of Him Who woke the dead.

" O Father of the fatherless, to Thee
    We turn, sole Comforter, and seek release,
When shall Thy better Kingdom come—and we
    Be gather'd 'neath Thy feet, and be at peace ?

Thou giv'st and tak'st away, Thy Name be blest !
    Fain would we have that Cup to pass away,
But may Thy will be done ; our only rest
    To know that Thou art good, and to obey.

Thy will be done on Earth, as 'tis in Heaven,
    Give us enough each day to bear us on ;
'Tis not our home, and as we have forgiv'n,
    Forgive us ere we die for Thy dear Son.

Look on us, for, like leaves, we haste away,
    And are not ; to Thy mercy let us cling :
Till we have pass'd this world of evil sway,
    Hide us beneath the shadow of Thy wing."

## X.

Thus hallow'd in Thy house of Prayer
Each change, else leading to despair,
Doth, like a pillar, heav'nward rise,
On which are built our destinies.
    I thank Thee, oft as we are there
And stand on the celestial stair,
Thy words the key-note still return,
Lest all too bold our fancies burn.

As " Holiness " on Aaron's head,
Which o'er his purple garments shed
That felt but untold sanctity
Of him who bears the Priestly key,
O'ershadowing with awe profound
Unto his tuneful skirts around.[1]
    Or as on Aaron's holier breast
The glorious constellations rest,
Enfolding " Light and Truth "[2] from high,
The voice of God in mystery.
Thus o'er each worship here below,
A light divine that Prayer doth throw.
    If 'neath the Church's parent shade
'Tis thus transform'd to meet our aid,
How shall it not abide the proof
For every want 'neath mortal roof !
O thought too high for mortal sense,
The lowliness, the confidence,
Reposing love, retiring fear,
Unspeakably combining there !
Within the wayside leaf, or flower,
Is hid a temple of strange power,
Of order fair a very world
Beneath a vein'd envelope curl'd,
All wondrous hid in viewless bars,
Like a blue night of silver stars.
'Tis thus where'er Thy hand hath been,
Tho' oft by none but Angels seen :
And here, conceal'd from careless eyes,
In sheltering veils there folded lies,
Within that Heaven-made prayer enroll'd,
Simplicity most manifold !
    Forms which surround Truth's secret throne
By varied name to mortals known,
    Are here united all in one ;
The Eight that hold the heavenly door,
Beatitudes of Gospel lore ;
The number'd Graces which all lie
In bosom of true Charity ;
The Fruits which round the branches twine,

[1 " Tuneful," because bells were hung on the hem of the garment.]
[2] Urim and Thummim. δήλωσις καὶ ἀλήθεια. Septuagint.

And gather o'er the mystic Vine,[1]
Like fairest shapes, unchang'd above,
   Yet altering their mien and air,
Throw varying shadows as they move
   O'er sunny earth and waters fair.
Within this Prayer come from on high,
Their embryo forms in secret lie,—
Here are the roots which all supply.
Like that dread image from the skies,
Before and after having eyes ;—
Or like a cloud, with lustre sown,
Where stars of the celestial zone
Blend in a bright communion.
   O hidden wisdom, ever nigh,
Then let me school mine ear and eye
To unwind all thy harmony.
'Tis ever thus in holy things,
The more we seek the sacred springs,
More fresh and deep their bounty flows,
More calm beneath the skies repose.
Oft'ner we turn, more love we learn,
And loving more, more thither turn.
For Prayer doth feeble Faith repair,
And Faith repair'd doth kindle Prayer ;
Like Angel forms on either hand,
They hold the Pilgrim thro' life's strand,
From strength to strength both leading on
In holy wondrous union.
Thus lifting up our thoughts on high,
We nearer bring the starry sky,—
E'en thus for ever newly born
Advancing into Heavenly morn.


## XI.

   Blest words come from the holiest shrine,
Ye that on Jesus' lips divine,
Ye that with Saints from age to age
Have been throughout their pilgrimage !
In triumph and in agony

---

[1] See Mr Miller's Sermons, Note to Sermon V.

Ye went between them and the sky,—
A road where aiding Angels came ;
May we in you partake their flame,
Bond of strange union when we kneel,
Think as they thought, and with them feel,
With Saints on earth and Saints on high,
Bound in mysterious sympathy !
By day and night there may we flee,
As to a sheltering sanctuary,
The refuge of a Father's name
Which only doth abide the same.

   Thro' life, as change and chance succeed,
That Prayer to Heaven doth bear our need,
And with Thine inspiration warm
Turns our dead thoughts to living form :
As when goes forth thy quickening breath,
Kindling the wrecks and dust of Death
Into the shapes of varied Life,
Trees, flowers, and streams, all beauty rife,—
Man, beast, and bird, one kindred strife,—
Earth, Sea, and Sky, uniting raise
A living temple to Thy praise.

   Thus have our earthly wishes turn'd
To wings that have with glory burn'd,
Fann'd into pure serene desires,
They clothe them with celestial fires,
Borne on the breath of our own Lord,
And instinct with the living Word,
But unto what shall we compare
The boundless hopes embosom'd there ?

   How beauteous here the Moon at night
Walks forth amid her hosts of light ;
And Evening looks, a pilgrim sage,
Out of his western hermitage ;
And Earth and Sea, whose voices rise
In solemn and dread harmonies ;
Then what shall be the spirit's home,
When Thy true Kingdom shall have come ?

   If in the flower such beauty lies,
Which blooms at morn, at evening dies ;
And in each form of life around
Mysterious wisdom hides profound ;

What shall our heavenly bodies be
When cloth'd with immortality?
    If in Thy guiding hand above
The glorious hosts are seen to move,
And all creation here below
Thy daily ordering seems to know;
How much more Thine unseen control
Must be around the human soul,
Prepar'd, beyond the starry skies,
To put on endless destinies!

## XII.

    I said, as change and chance succeed,
That Prayer doth Heaven-ward bear our need,—
When in this temple, greenly dight,[1]
And arch'd o'er with its roof of light,
Our childhood woke to earth's unrest,
That Prayer came like an Angel guest,
And in that pensive silent cell,
Which heart of childhood knoweth well,
It led our thoughts by gentle mien
To dwell around a Friend unseen;
And turn'd from earth the wondering eyes
Unto a happier Paradise.
    When we were grown to riper years,
Woo'd by a world of hopes and fears,
Each morn and evening it would come,
And lighting up the silent room
Would oft forgotten still intrude
On evening's holier solitude,
A gentle witness standing nigh
Of things that should not be put by.
    More and more to our manlier sense
Faith's treasur'd stores it doth dispense,
A key that opes omnipotence:
It can the mountains set afar,
Which our obedience seem to bar.
But if not made in love our own

[1 "Greenly dight." The earth as it appears to us in our youth is clothed with spring loveliness.]

It is a witness of stern tone ;
Or seems with parting wings to go,
And leave us to the world below.
When age hath come, ere we depart,
That witness takes the Judge's part,—
The Judge's part, which serves to prove
Thoughts chain'd below, or train'd above,
Of character the form and measure,
Of our desires, our hope, and treasure :
Whether in converse with the sky
We strength have gain'd to walk on high ;
With thoughts to our true Father led,
Content below with daily bread :
Or whether in low dreams of earth
Forgotten lies our better birth.


## XIII.

Thro' life, as change and chance succeed,
It thus doth vary to our need,
And to the faith-illumin'd sense
Expandeth its magnificence.
Said I, 'twas like the silver Moon,
Companion thro' night's wintry noon ?
Yea, and I deem it not too bold,
Could I its treasures half unfold :
"Tis fraught with goodness all Thine own,
Whilst Thou, our Sun, from sight art gone.
Lo, earth-born cares are at its rising riven,
And wither'd hopes have caught the holier hues of Heaven !
    Said I, 'twas like the solemn Sea,
So simple in sublimity,
Transform'd to meet each changing scene,
And glass Heaven's face dark or serene ?
Man's hand hath been on all beside,
Thy holy footsteps there abide,
Tho' all too deep for mortal pride.
In that baptismal flood serene
Still would I wash, and still be clean.
    Said I, 'twas like a constant Friend,
Whom we would hold when life shall end

Yea, it shall ever be to me
In solitude best company :
And a sweet spell when friends are nigh,
A presence felt in silence by.
Yea, while we walk with cloud and shade,
And meteor lights our path invade,
Let not a wish within me burn,
But first unto that Prayer I turn !
And, oh, may I at life's dim close
Know of that Prayer the calm repose !

## The Middle Aisle.

*Holy Scripture.*

———

Our mirror is a blessed book,
   Where out from each illumin'd page
We see one glorious image look
   All eyes to dazzle and engage.
               *The Christian Year.*

### I.

"A LITTLE further lend Thy guiding hand,"
A little onward, Heaven-descended Guide!
This scene will soon be o'er, where Hope and Fear
Busily twine the thread of hurrying life;
And this strange house, where the o'er-arching blue
Bends o'er us, from whose dark aerial caves
The Day and Night, on Time's alternate watch,
In solemn interchanges come and go,
And Winter and swift Summer hasten by
So stilly; soon its portal will be past,—
E'en now my shadow on the mountain side
Is lengthening,—hues of Evening o'er me fall.
   Thy guiding hand a little further on,
Whate'er Thou art that thro' unravelling time
Leadest me on! for oft Thy hand I feel,
And tho' amid life's solitudes I droop
Unmindful, oft beside me in the gloom,
And oft'ner still behind, 'mid travell'd scenes

As back I bear my view, celestial tracks
I see, and "skirts of an unearthly friend."
　Yet not so much, that, while I wondering tread
Th' unfoldings of Thy silent Providence,
Thou giv'st to feel Thy kind withholding chain,
And gentle leading ;—not so much for this,
I thank Thee, heavenly Father, Friend, and Lord,
As that each morn and eve, that hasten on
My days to number, to the homeless heart,
Which turns from fairest scenes unsatisfied,
Wearied with vain pursuits, and vainer end,
Thou in serener dwellings dost disclose
The Kingdom of Thy treasures, new and old.
—Oft some arm'd Saint, who saw th' Invisible,
And in that strength bore heathen gates away,
Or swordless slew the giant ;—oft deep thoughts
Revealing, in Thy Gospel's bosom laid.
　Thus may Thy Church within her daily arms
Take me, and with her blessing let me go,—
But not with her depart her accents sweet.
Thus be my loins girded with holier hope,
And discipline, and penitential thought,
Led by the hand of self-rewarding care.
Nor know I aught beside to buoy the soul
Against the weight of her own solitude,
Aim-less and object-less ; or, what is worse,
Fever'd pursuit, and restless followings on
Of the impassion'd being, meteor lights
Which leave at last to deeper loneliness.
　Thence is the soul attun'd to secret spells
Of that eternal music heard in Heaven,
Albeit hush'd by ruder sounds of earth,
Yet pure and deep as the celestial spheres,
Which calm the wayward spirit, and reveal
Other pursuits, and ends which end not here ;
A light that brighter burns unto the close ;
A feeling of immortal youth within,
That while these earthly weeds and flowery hopes
Drop from us, looks to an enduring home ;
A sense of reconcilement oft renew'd,
And power to throw aside the darts of care,
Temptation-proof, ethereal panoply.

## II.

Thy guiding hand a little further on !
Thus doth Thy spirit walk with soundless tread
In the outgoings of the morn and eve,
Leading us on, unseen, unheard of man :
Constant—as dews whose footsteps fall from Heaven,
Noiseless, and not less balmy in their tread ;
Gradual—as rays that build the golden grain ;
Unseen—as gales that homeward bear the sail ;
Dear—as awaken'd thoughts of absent home ;
And soothing—as familiar strains from far,
Long-lov'd, but dull to unaccustom'd ear.
  And sweet it were to steal from day to day
From the rude thoughts and fever of the world,
To sit upon that mighty river's bank,
Descending from the everlasting hills :
To travel on its banks, and watch the flow
Untouch'd by man, making free melodies,
With multitudinous waters as it goes :—
Such is Thy word, which thro' our annual round
Flows on its course, unfolding more and more,
And gladdening scenes of life, which hath its spring
Beneath the throne of God, and lingers not,
But to th' eternal ocean passes on.

## III.

Mysterious deeps of wisdom, dimly known,
Where fathom of man's thought ne'er touch'd the ground,
Who shall thy lessons reach, who shall descry
His steps of light, Who in His boundless word
The wilderness of waters walks unseen ?
In this Thy visible house, mankind's abode,
Thy hand withdraws from search of human ken,
Whene'er the depths we trace, there opes beyond
An inner world, where Science lifts her torch,
And Wonder leads thro' dim enchanted halls,
And glorious links we see of heavenly mould,
But cannot track the chain ; Thyself, unseen,
Sittest behind the mighty wheel of things,
Which moves harmonious, tho' unheard below,
Save when Thine order'd ways, at interval,

Break forth, as falling on some traveller's ear
Musical notes, which make the landscape smile.
　The Hand that kindles up the rolling moon,
Lights up the worm's blue lamp beside our path ;
And haply in Thy word there hidden lies
Infinity, coil'd up in narrowest bound ;
We on the surface walk, and know it not.
　The bird, that sits and sings upon the thorn,
Knows not its Maker's wonders, known to man :
Man moves 'mid hidden things, to Angels known,
Nor knows of aught, around, above, beneath,
Where'er he turns, beside the path of life,
Enough on earth to know.—O send Thou forth
Thy Light and Truth from Thine unseen abodes,
That they may lead me to Thy Holy Hill.
Thou that hast made the heart and seeing eye,
Give me to know Thyself, of all things else
Let me be ignorant deem'd ; for Thee to know
Is to know all that's good, and fair below ;—
Without Thee we are blind, but in Thee see
Thy multitude of mercy far and wide,
Thee good in all, and all things good in Thee.
Thee only none can seek and seek in vain ;
Thus travelling thro' the world's lone desert way,[1]
If, with that Ethiop stranger, o'er Thy word
I bend, Thy Heaven-sent guide is at my side.


IV.

Thy guiding light a little further on !
Shower on my heart Thy radiance, without which
Thine own sure word were but a barren void,
But ever and anon, as Thy calm light
Falls on it, Thy deep fulness comes to view.
Oft clouds and darkness all about Thee dwell,
Till thoughts responsive wake with changeful life,
And open all Thy word, as light or shade
Fall on it, and fresh scenes arise to light,
With life and infinite variety,
Ever unfolding, as in scenes of Earth,

[1] Acts viii. 26.

Mountains, and plains, and streams, and land, and sea.
As when upon a wild autumnal noon,
Some traveller sits on airy cliffs, and sees
The far-spread range below, where lights and shades
In beauteous interchanges come and go.
One scene comes forth to view, another fades,
Trees on a distant line—then gleaming rocks,
And woods, dwellings of men, and 'tween the hills
O'er-arching, haply gleams the opening sea,
And some lone bark in sunshine—then retires
In shade—the nearer object comes to light
Unseen before—and then on either side
The multifarious landscape breaks to sight,
Unseen, till the bright beam expands the view.
Thus the unbounded fulness of Thy word
Betokens Thy dread Glory veil'd beneath,
Throwing the light and cloud Thy skirts around.
   Lend me Thy hand, celestial visitant,
Into the inner chambers where Thou sitt'st
Unfolding lessons of diviner lore !
Touch'd by th' unearthly wand, ethereal doors
Fly open, answering to the wondrous key.
I seem behind this shifting scene of things
Admitted, Heaven's high counsels to behold.
I seem to wander thro' mysterious ways,—
Shadows of other days, and other lights
Around me,—such is Thy unfathom'd word ;
And oft at every turn myself descry.
Patriarchs, and Kings, and Prophets, great and good,
Are hurrying all before us to the tomb,
And cry aloud, "We seek another home."
I seem to walk through Angel-haunted caves,
Lit by celestial light, not of the Sun,
That leadeth to a kingdom far away.
There as behind this screen, and sensual bar,
I see a Hand that weighs us day by day,
We, wrapt in earthly schemes are hastening on,
And heed not ; while Thy Judgments walk the earth,
Evils by mortals nam'd, and Mercy loves
Beneath a cloud to veil her silver wings,
To me still speaks Thy voice, myself I see,
I see myself in each new scene reveal'd.

## V.

Thy guiding hand a little further on !
Now Death on the new world in twilight dim
Alighting, spreads his wings from pole to pole ;
Lo, as the wily Tempter coils away,
I hide me from my sins in coverts green,
And think Thine eye beholds not, but Thy voice,
'Mid the dread stillness of the evening's close,—
Thy sternly-kind enquiring voice I hear :
In wither'd and vile leaves I stand reveal'd.
Anon a beckoning hand I see afar,
It is the call that came to Terah's son,
Singling me out from old Euphrates' bank,
And bids me follow to a land unknown.
I linger on, and hear not, but afar
I see the holy Abraham journeying on
Unto that heavenly Canaan, now awhile
He leans on Haran's tomb,[1] now westward wends
Unto the unseen City, built of God.
Strong in celestial hope he walks on high,
In Heaven-conversing solitude ; that sight
Girds me with other strength, but loitering still
Myself I see at every turn disclos'd,
Wooing fair phantoms.   He is travelling on
He knows not whither, but serene and glad,
Rests with no meaner things, no servant-heir
Chosen awhile, but lifts his eyes aloft
Unto the unseen City, built of God.


## VI.

Now like a widening river opes the scene ;
A flying host is seen, and marvellous way,
And sea on either hand, with watery walls.
Heaven hath come down, and with life-giving touch
Struck all the desert ; there where Nature pin'd,
She hath forgot herself, and looks around—
Rocks gushing, Angel's food, the light, and cloud,
The mountain mantled round with fire and smoke,
And terrible voice.   'Tis desolate around,

[1] Gen. xi. 28.]

And far below stretches that livid sea,
Where o'er his black domain the vulture sails
To mountains far away, bright fruitful lands,
Where God would bear them upon eagle's wings,
But Israel turns away, and fears, and pines !

It is the Christian thro' life's wilderness
Numbering his forty years, and Mercy's form
Stretching her arms. 'Tis desolate around,
But with new hopes Heaven opens in the wild,
We knowing know not, but to Egypt turn.

Like that fam'd Trojan in the Tyrian hall [1]
Who 'mid the pictur'd host himself descried,
I start—and see myself in stern review.
And lo, all life seems teeming with new thoughts,
And other purposes ordain'd of old !
I thread a path replete with embryo life,
Unwinding golden destinies, and oft
Find me in a mysterious balance weigh'd.

What are these washings, ceremonial chains,
And all this flow of sacrificial blood?
The Holiest of Holies open stands,
On that dread sorrowing Sabbath, which gives life
To all the year, the great Atoning Day.—
Christian, thou tread'st on solemn mysteries,
Strange prophecies, and counsels laid in Heaven ;
Dim clues, which thro' Life's winding labyrinth
Lead on, emerging in ethereal day,
If Wisdom lend her kind conducting hand.

To my dark steps a little further on !
Now Israel sits in Canaan's promis'd rest,
The Lord like His own mountains stands around ;
But sounds of arms are on the distant gale ;
He sits,—but by his side his sword and shield.
Before, an armed Angel leads the way,
But Superstition's haggard brow, behind,
Gleams darkly, by each hill and green tree's shade,
While fitfully breaks forth the wandering moon
On Canaan's fallen towers.  Is this the rest ?—
I start and look around me—
                    This the land,
Ordain'd of old, the glad Inheritance?

[1] Æneid, b. i. 488.

The Peace beneath the Gospel's sheltering vine?
The heavenly kingdom?   Mammon reigneth here;
And Passion's sevenfold host of Canaan born!
Amid a falling world we build again
Their idol temples!   Thence arise to view
Times heavy with dark signs, and days of old,
And Noah stretching forth beseeching hands,
Fearfully seen the type of darker days;[1]
Judgment is at the door, and even now
With the dread Coming gleams the Eastern gate,
We plant, and build, and hearing, hear it not.


## VII.

Thy guiding hand a little further on,
Into the treasures of Thine inner shrine!
O perfect energy of Thy deep word,
With varied ends combining all in one,
Like nature's works, all one, all manifold!
Each hath its single lesson, each is part
Of one great whole, that whole in each is found,
Each part with th' other blends, and lends its light.
One perfect whole, where earth and sea and skies
Are mirror'd; now at random thrown apart,
In thousand scintillations far and wide,
Each fragment bears the earth and sea and skies,
Each on the other throws its pictur'd form,
And all combine in one mysterious whole.
    There Wisdom varies oft her mien and form,
Now sits with Job, bow'd down to misery's chain;
Wonderful things from water, earth, and air,
Approach her in the dismal solitude,—
A wilderness all touch'd by fiery breath—
The thunder and the lightning come to him,
The Behemoth is there, and mightiest forms
From the dark lair of Nature's hiding-place
Come forth, to speak their Maker mightier far.
There Patience sits, and drooping Penitence,
That long had sought, and vainly sought relief,

---

[1] As it was in the days of Noe, so shall it be also in the days of the Son of Man.—St Luke xvii. 26.

Her image eyes in Woe's black flowing stream,
And lifts her head by bitterness reviv'd.
  The scene is chang'd, and Wisdom by the gate
Sits calling to the simple ones ; and now
Her precepts are link'd beads of many hues,
She bears the golden key to hidden stores,
Rubies, and health, and plenteous barns, and wine,
A crown of glory, or a sheltering shield,
Apples of gold in silver pictures laid,
Wherein the Gospel's light in secret burns,
A tree of life, an ever-brightening path,
Now length of days, now ways of pleasantness,
Now one that in an ivory palace dwells,
Now terrors in her hand, and hell and death,
Now in the whirlwind walks an armed man.[1]
Thus, like the face of the autumnal night,
She varies ; lo, anon her son she brings
On the world's highest stair, experience-crown'd :[2]
O Royal Preacher, wondrous is thy voice,
And deep thy tale of human vanity,
Of nothing true but God, nor calm but Heaven !


## VIII.

  Thy guiding hand a little further on !
What visionary shapes now fill the gloom,[3]
Of more than earthly wisdom, tho' in grief
O'er earthly things they hang their drooping form?
And who art thou with robes all rudely rent,
Sitting beneath the lofty Lebanon,
Thy realm a waste, and Solitude thy throne?
Daughter of Salem, from what gate of strength
Descending, sitt'st thou at the door of Death?
And can our God cast off His own elect?
Desolate Judah, lesson sad to us !
Desolate Judah, sitting on the ground !
O thou, but little 'mid the nations known
In arts or arms, (emblem of Hope divine
By man despis'd,) O thou, but little known
In arts or arms, but better known of God,—

---

[1] The Proverbs.     [2] Ecclesiastes.     [3] The Prophets.

And could not this content thee, little one?
Euphrates' bank, and Chebar's distant flood,
Have echoed to thy Jordan's deep lament.
  Now all is vocal with prophetic strains,
And Lebanon and Carmel find a voice,
Kingdoms their mighty shadows cast before
Going to ruin—Tyre, and Nineveh,
And Babylon.   Behind the fleeting scene
Stern Retribution sits, and holds the scale,
Where empires all are weigh'd, rebellious Pride
With meteor lamp leads on to dusky Death.
  Meanwhile, as flows the stream of mortal things,
There riseth up the mist of human woes,
And, lo, that mist is skirted with the gleam
Which harbingers the slowly-rising morn,
And brightens more and more, as darker grows
The gather'd cloud, until effulgent made
With rays prophetic purpling all the dawn,
Lo, it reveals the Sun of Righteousness,
Streaming in light o'er the dim vale of life,
And hills of immortality afar.


## IX.

  Thy guiding hand a little further on!
Now other ears we need, and other eyes,
For semblance hath brought forth reality :
The cloud the Sun, the night reveal'd the Day,[1]
Which from her open'd portals walks abroad,
With messages of mercy to the poor.
The volume is unfolded day by day,
Unletter'd hinds are greater than the proud,
And penniless old age is rich and young,
Sequester'd ignorance is wiser far
Than knowledge, in her city trappings dress'd.
See, where combin'd in our diurnal round,
There moves a twofold orb of light divine,[2]

---

[1 The birth of Christ is the birth of the Day after dark night.]
[2] The Daily Lessons.

And throws th' united gleam upon our path,
Morning and Eve, lightening the narrow way.
 Thy guiding hand a little further on !
All things are now made new, another Sun
Shines o'er us, and another Moon from high,
Each passing day reveals a sacred step,
Where thro' life's cave our Lord the burden bore ;
And when receiv'd into a golden cloud
Thy form is seen no more, Thy sacred voice
In Apostolic warnings cloth'd anew
Is heard, as oft as Evening Shadows fall.[1]
 Thy guiding hand a little further on !
Man hath gone down unto a cheerless tomb,
Dismays and doubts around, and all before
Peopled with visionings of his sad mind,
Doubting of good because deserving ill,
Scarce daring to believe God's mercy true
When broke the Church amid the shining Heavens
With all her saints array'd in Jesus' robe,
Rejoicing in the light of other worlds,
Beyond the dull house of mortality.
As when one on a nightly journey wends
With clouded Heavens around him, till from high
Far on her nightly tower is seen the Moon,
With one pale glimmering star,—then hills afar
Come forth in brightness, promontories, seas,
And hanging woods, and gradual breaks to view
The infinite expanse, and all the stars ;
He on his homeward way rejoicing goes.
 A little onward lend thy guiding hand !
Thus daily may we gather better thoughts,
And arm our souls with steadfastness, or learn
That we have nought to gather, nought to lose,
On earth, and in that knowledge learn our peace.
Then welcome disappointment, and decay,
Bereavement, and keen sense of lov'd ones lost,—
While not a star along the aerial hall,
But solitude, and sterner forms of woe
Lend their companionship amid the gloom—
Full welcome, if they lead us, in Thy path,
To cling the more to Thy parental hand,

[1] The Evening Lesson.

Far better than false gleams that lead us thence,
And then desert us.
                              Soon comes forth to view
Upon her nightly watch the silent Moon,
Ether's blue arms around her, gradual breaks
The infinite expanse, and all the stars ;
He on his homeward way rejoicing goes.
    Then by degrees is gathered that within,
Which more and more impels, and urges on
Heavenward—himself unconscious of the Power ;
Like gales that swell unseen, and move at length
The unheeding bark, or thoughts the unconscious frame.
Thence he the spirit of obedience wears,
Chains round the neck, and ornaments of grace,
By others seen, but to himself unknown,
Blest ignorance, the nurse of lowly thoughts !


## X.

    A little onward lend Thy guiding hand !
The Sun now rises on the Minaret, [1]
And desolation lingers o'er the walls,
Where Angels once, like its own mountain band,
Stood round Jerusalem ; thro' that blest realm
Scarce doth a sacred track unharm'd remain,
At Nazareth's lone hill-side, or silent lake,
(Dear lake, dear hills, where Thy blest eyes repos'd !)
But in the living page Thy steps abide,
Fresh as of yesterday.   Faith lights her lamp,
And rising thence she sees thee all around ;
She walks the earth, in amice of the morn,
And wheresoe'er the need of human woe
Varies its shape, she finds Thee standing nigh,
And burns to follow.   Oft Thy presence lies
Hidden in busy scenes, but as they pass,
The parting step reveals Thy form Divine,

[1 He contemplates the Holy Land, now given over to the Moslem.
Yet Faith looking beyond the visible, sees Christ still, thinks of the past
Divine Acts which these scenes witnessed, and remembers that He
remains the same for ever.]

And gentle dealings : as we backward bear
The thoughtful eye, we see in vision clear,
And lost occasions mourn.   Oh, that we thence
Might gain th' enduring sense of Thy deep love,
How in that light would things terrestrial wear
Celestial colourings, that we no more
Should droop, or in Thy Presence feel alone !
    Thy guiding hand a little further on !
As when, amid her azure palaces,
Mounts in her solemn state the Queen of night,
Her airy pathway holds the floating web,
Shook from her brow the silver clouds among :
So doth Thy solemn memory here remain.
Not now beheld at Abraham's friendly door,
In flaming bush, or Gideon's threshing-floor,
As man with man, or wrapt with Angel wings ;
Not now beside the Galilean shore ;
But where the widow'd mother walks bereav'd,
Where Poverty and Blindness by the way,
Where Innocence sits at the festal board,
Or listening Penitence hangs down to mourn.
    Lend me Thy light a little further on !
Henceforth the Church is as the living shrine,
Wherein the Angel of Thy presence dwells,
About Thee thrown like an illumin'd cloud.
She hand in hand with morning issues forth,
And daily traversing the peopled globe
Kindles mute forms, in which her Spirit dwells,
Circling the earth with her celestial day,
As with a radiant zone, while from her steps
Night flies : she on her path continuous wakes
Her ancient prayers, and David's holy song,
From Ganges' bank to these cold Western isles.
    Nor only thus, but veil'd in silvery mist
With each she springs from the Baptismal fount,
And half disclosing her celestial brow,
She lends herself companion of the way,
Seizing the trembler's hand, and seeing things
He sees not, forward leads him thro' the night,
And tries him oft in crooked and dark ways
Of discipline, and penitential love,
Till with her secrets she can trust his soul.

## XI.

To my dark steps a little further on,
As things here seen on earth—the Night—the Storm,—
The Thunder—Pain—Unrest—and pale Remorse,
Girding around with ever-during fire,
And boding evil; so within Thy word
Dark auguries in terror seem to walk,
And sterner premonitions blend with hope,
The dread forerunners of the Judgment-morn.
Let not these pass, like clouds which summer gilds,
Lest shapes sublime and shadowy semblances
Teach us th' o'erwhelming substance to forego;
Lest flowers, which spring around the fount of truth,
We gather for frail wreaths of poesy,
Nor know our foulest selves reflected there.
Lest of these mighty things we talk and feel
Unprofited, and fail the will to do;—
The tabernacle deck with curious art,
Forget the engraven word laid up within,
Nor know the mercy-seat, and awful cloud.
  Thy guiding hand a little further on!
The Day and Night on their alternate watch,
And Time's bright sentinels that walk the sky,
The Sun and Moon—'tis written, doubt it not—
Shall pass, and in the darkness make their bed:
And we unloos'd out from this womb of things
Shall on the mighty stair of Being climb.
  Unto the light a little further on!
Day after day that book is open laid,
A day shall come, and cannot now be far,
A day shall come, when last it shall be seen,—
The universe, of Angels and of men,
Shall stand around, and Christ Himself shall sit
Upon the great tribunal, plac'd on high,
And then that book shall be reopen'd wide,
And we shall look upon the Judge's face,
And on that book—and then shall hear His voice.

## XII.

  Thy guiding hand a little further on!
O Thou sole End and Author of all hope,

That hast reveal'd the sinner's dwelling-place,
And the eternity of Heaven and Hell,
Look on us, teach us upon Thee to lean ;
O'er the dread gulf disclose Thy peaceful path !
For Thou art not in brain-sick ecstasy,
That climbs the Heavens to light th' unhallowed torch
Fever'd Imagination's fiery wing,
Like vap'rous breath, which in the furnace mounts,
Fann'd to a vitreous blaze, and hangs again
In earth-born vapour on the vault above ;
But in that viewless flame, from ashes born
Of Penitence, with lowlier wisdom wise,
Born to a purer love, and onward bent
To purge terrestrial dross, that trembling still
In thankfulness, in lowliness, and love,
With Anna and with Simeon, good of old,
Waits in Thy courts : while still, from step to step,
On stair by Israel seen, dwindle behind
The towers of earth, and gradual grow before
The immensities of Heaven.   Oh, lend me wings,
Ethereal Spirit, ere that stair of Heaven
Be gather'd up into th' enfolding clouds,
And I be left in darkness,—low I sit—
In sorrow,—penitence-strick'n, and deep woe,—
'Mid shades of Death, Thine arrow drinks my blood.
For I Thine innocent side have pierced deep,
For I have pierced deep Thine innocent side,
Thou Holy One, and I could sit and weep,
But that Thou bidd'st me rise, and with Thy voice
Of ever-varying seasons, day and night,
And this eternity that stirs within,
Thou bidd'st us stand not, but arise, and wash
Our robes to meet Thee, and to trim the lamp.
Bow'd with the o'erwhelming burden down to earth,
I dared not look upon Thy bleeding brow ;
Like some poor Alpine wanderer, who in dreams,
In powerless dreams, beholds th' incumbent pile,
Heavily overhanging—threat'ning still,
Still threat'ning to hurl down the gather'd Alp ;
But now I trembling look to Thee, and, oh,
If not to me the harp of Jesse's son,
Which bade the gloomy spirit part from Saul,

In blooming-hair'd youth ; oh, for that harp,
With which in later day, with sackcloth rob'd
And Penitence, his overcharged heart
Broke forth, and gave its sorrows to the strings,
Of deep-ingrained guilt—of guilt that cleaves
Unto the bone of life.   Thee shall I sing,
While passion round the heart with snaky wile
Wreathes its dark folds, and pride, that foully feeds
On praise of man, breeding distemper'd blood,
And dons the pilgrim's cowl and lowly weed !
Wash me again for Thine, and bind my wounds,
For whom have I in Heaven but Thee alone?
And whom on earth—but Thee? and well I know
If I dare lean on aught but Thee alone,
I mourn a broken reed and bleeding side.
    Oh, lead me but a little further on !
Oh, now, I now behold Thee, who thou art,
Celestial Visitant ! I see Thee now
Confess'd, and my revealed God adore !          •
Stay with me, for the evening goes away ;
I am not worthy Thou beneath my roof
Should'st enter—if Thou enterest not, I die ;
The day is now far spent, and evening shades
Are coming on—oh, with me stay awhile !

## The South Aisle.

### The Creed.

I. *The vastness of the Creed.* II. *Its all-pervading charity.* III. *How to be impressed with its importance.* IV. *The same.* V. *Unsatisfying nature of earthly things.* VI. *The Creed paraphrased, as our only consolation.* VII. *The stronghold of Faith.* VIII. *In the Occasional Services.* IX. *The proportion of Faith.* X. *How received into the soul.* XI. *Its practical effects.* XII. *A Prayer to hold it aright, and find rest therein.*

---

The greater height these Graces reach,
The clearer they the mystery teach ;
Saints best in their own souls may read
The illustration of their Creed.

*Kenn*, vol. i. 269.

### I.

Go, stand beneath some Minster tall,
Stretching in aisles majestical ;
In branchings of embowering length,
And avenues of pillar'd strength,
'Mid arch and pile aloft array'd,
And clustering reach of vaulted shade,
Dwarf'd to a speck man there doth stand,
'Mid the colossal mountain band.
  Or go, and gaze, when mortals sleep,
Upon the wild ethereal deep !
Solemn and vast in night's stern dress,
Of worlds a very wilderness,
In their blue caves half seen they lie,
The many mansions of the sky.
Man sinks his inmost soul within,
In littleness and conscious sin.
  Thus, in Christ's holy Creed displayed,
Truth on eternal pillars laid,
World beyond world, end without end,
Doth over man her vastness bend.
Far stooping from the deeps of night,
She stands reveal'd to mortal sight,
Like the broad Heaven's o'er-arching span,
Divinity encircling man.

## II.

What is the long Cathedral glade,
But Faith that in the structur'd shade,
Herself embodies to the sense,
Leaning upon Omnipotence ;
And Holiness, ennobling thought,
Into a living temple wrought ?
There Strength and Beauty spring to life,
In contests of harmonious strife ;
With blended glories high aloof,
Embracing on the gorgeous roof,
Till standing 'neath the giant throng
The soul expands, and feels her strong
With more than doth to man belong.
    Nor gazing on th' ethereal hall,
Let thoughts of vastness thee appal !
Through the still arch, Night's awful dome,
Love gleams from his eternal home,
With countenance unearthly bright
Lifting the curtains of dead Night,
And thro' the vast of that wild sea
Speaks peace to fall'n humanity.
E'en thus the Creed's eternal scroll
Doth awe, but not confound the soul ;
Like tent of ether spread above,
All fostering, all sustaining Love,
There stretches her unfailing strength,
And height, and depth, and breadth, and length,
Doth to our aid itself unfold,
Exalt, ennoble, strengthen, hold,
'Neath whose encircling canopy
We may from Sin and Sorrow flee.
God the beginning whence it rose,
And everlasting life the close.
    Tho' clouds and darkness mantle round
Those towers, disclos'd on heavenly ground,
Mercy with them her light is blending,
On embassies of grace descending.
    There, as within a darken'd glass,
Our God before us deigns to pass,

We 'neath His sheltering hand may hide,
And in our Rock unharm'd abide.
   No sooner in His might array'd,
He hath the world's foundations laid,
Holding in hollow of His hand,
The Heavens—and earth—and sea—and land,
When lo, the crystal skies descend,[1]
He comes below of man the Friend,
To walk with man till time shall end—
In him, with him, the weary steep to climb,
And lead him to calm heights beyond the sea of time.

### III.

   Good Angels, I would fain adore,
And trace the secrets of your shore,
In safety guide my feeble bark,
And lift the mantle of the dark !
How bring we near to mortal eyes
Those infinite realities,
That they may on our spirits dwell,
The Great, the Good, th' unchangeable !
   Upon the glass the creeping fly
Will shut out mightiest worlds on high,
And care, to earthly projects given,
Will hide from man his God and Heaven.
   'Tis distance dwarfs the mighty star,
In Night's blue caves scarce seen afar,
But the great God to us is near,
As mortal eye, or mortal ear,
And that vast sea, which knows no shore,
With all its floods is at the door.
   'Tis in the holy Liturgy
We come to sit its margin nigh,
Till haply so familiar grown,
With glorious things to man made known,
We by that standard rightly scan
How little, and how great is man.
   It is the soul in love and fear,
Kindling to life th' eternal sphere,

---

[1] *I.e.*, as the Creed proceeds.

Till mightiest things that fill the sky,
And walk in immortality,
Assemblages of light around,
Wakening throughout the dim profound,
All tremblingly begin to stir,
A living amphitheatre,
Where Jesus 'mid the dark serene
O'er the vast circuit walks unseen.
    'Tis Thoughtfulness on brooding wing,
Earth's lowliest duties cherishing,
And Prayer that bringeth down the skies
With dread immortal companies.
    Thus in Thy hallow'd house on earth,
Breathing the breath of our new birth,
As thro' a portal we descry,
Growing upon the gazing eye,
The palace of eternity.
    Without, forgetful we are Thine,
We seek for happiness, and pine,
There, in the ocean of Thy love,
Remember that in Thee we move,
And breathe the life-restoring air
Of Thy calm presence ;—earthly care
Looses her hold ; Faith more and more
Admits to her celestial store.


IV.


Why dwells the lover on the glance
Of some endeared countenance ?
At each remembrance in him stirs
A man of strength, oft as recurs
Thought upon thought, a link remains,
Until the soul is found in chains.
    What binds the exile to his home ?
Regretful memories, that come
With images that love to dwell
By some known tree or native well.
    What weds the traitorous soul to gold ?
Cares which returning manifold
At morn and eve, grow on the soul,

And thence shut out the mighty whole,
Heaven's heights and everlasting goal.
  What lit in thee the lamp of love,
Great Saint of Patmos?  Thoughts above
Ever conversing with the Word,
In cherish'd memory seen and heard.
Thine eagle eye was ever bent
Gazing upon the firmament,
Till on thee burst th' ethereal world,
Armies of God with signs unfurl'd.
And thou wast seen 'mong men to be
The o'erflowing fount of charity.
  Thus Faith, her torch-light to repair,
Will oft return, and linger there,
Where Truth, unfolding her deep creed,
Opens the Heavens to meet our need,
And shews lights gleaming evermore,
  On margin of th' eternal shore.
  How shall I thank Thy Majesty,
That giv'st to know ourselves, and Thee ;—
The mercies which with Thee abide,
The littleness of all beside ;—
Not in the cloud spread forth above,
  Not in the light on Aaron's breast,
But in this mantle of Thy love,
  Which on each earthly scene doth rest !


## V.

Spirit of awe, my fancy lead,
While thus 'mid holy things I tread,
Lay on my lips Thy sweet control,
And touch them with the living coal !
  That Creed in the calm Liturgy,
'Mid varied worship, prayer, and praise,
Concentrating their heavenly rays,
  Is like the lamp that came from high,
And moved, beneath the nightly skies,
'Mid the divided secrifice.
Then spake a voice to Terah's son, [1]

[1] Genesis xv. 17.

' 'Mid foes, meek stranger, hold thee on,
' A little while—on either hand
'They shall be gone, but thou shalt stand.'
Sweet words of holy embassage,
May ye my weary soul engage,
In this my house of pilgrimage !
While watchful foes around me throng,
Make me in your blest wisdom strong !
   With throbbing head and aching breast,
I find no Elim's shade of rest.
   I wander 'neath this desert Sun,
Shod with desires still fresh and bold ;
My earthly weeds have not grown old,
    But here of good I nought have won,
    My hopes are yet where they begun.
    Pride came, and whisper'd secretly,
To come unto her nest on high :
There was a gleam that slumber'd there,
It was the storm's bright harbinger.
That calm—it was the thunder's shroud—
For sorrow aye pursues the proud.
    Peace came with tale of gentle springs,
Of valleys and sequesterings,
Where on the mirror of her breast,
Tranquilly I might lean and rest.
That vale was an unearthly land,
Guarded by some enchanted band,
Nor can I know that sweet recess,
Till friendly death shall me undress.
Then Friendship came with purest hope below,
Like dark-stoled Una with her Lamb of snow :
But, if to her I wed my days,
I should forget a holier praise !
Yet, so I loved the sacred grace,
And Angel calm of her dear face,
That I will leave her for a while,
To gain her everlasting smile.
    Ah, well I know thee, Solitude,
Thy silent cell and sinking mood ;
And hard the task with thee to dwell,
And love thy thoughtful citadel,
    But for the star that lights thy page,

And cheers thine evening hermitage.
   Then Learning tun'd her classic lute
So touchingly, the vale hung mute ;
I turn'd to seek one by my side,
But found not—there sat lonely Pride,
The heart still droop'd unsatisfied.
   Then Nature oped her hidden treasure,
Defying bound, defying measure,
With beauty half reveal'd, half shewn,
Still leading to her Lord unknown :
The soul amid the landscape fair,
For something sought which was not there.
   Then pointed she with iron hand
Unto Religion's calm abode ;
But gleams, that broke the twilight shew'd
   Dark Superstition's phantom band,
   Which round her cave were seen to stand.
Pale Care was there, to whom Heaven's bird
Sang her sweet lesson all unheard :
Distrust that scarce could light descry
'Mid tangled woods—felt none was nigh :
And wan Despair 'mid places lone
Brooding o'er that which Time hath done,
And Time can ne'er undo again ;—
Pharpar and Abana all vain,
Or Ocean's self to wash her stain.


## VI.

   The quiet of this Summer Eve,
When birds are on their homeward wing,
Save night's sweet friend that wakes to sing,
   Should soothe a heart unus'd to grieve.
But lights, that fall on yonder glade,
Do but disclose a darker shade,
And Nature in her joyous mood
Were but a deeper solitude,
But for the gleams of heavenly Love,
Which fall from our true home above.
   The shadow sleeps upon the hill,
In Nature's temple all is still.

With rippling stir the leaflets move,
Tho' not a gale to wake the grove ;
The lake hath caught a silver crest,
Tho' not a breath to break its rest.
Calm tremblings thro' the earth and sky
Speak some approaching Deity ;
    Shadows of earth hold me no more,
Ah, glorious light, I see thee now,
    Forth issuing from the eastern door,
I turn, and head and heart I bow.


## The Creed.

Do I believe in God above ?[1]
Then nought on earth my heart shall move,
    Calm I unravel life's dull lore,
That I may so His goodness prove.
    Away with sad distrust, no more
    Come knocking at my heart's low door !
What shall th' Almighty's power withstand,[2]
What shall withhold a Father's hand,
That hand which made and holds the sky and sea and shore ?

One only son within Thy breast,
In Jesus Christ made manifest,
    He is my Heaven-born earth-born Lord,[3]
I see Him and I find my rest ;
    Conceiv'd of Holy Ghost [4]—the Word,—
    Earth saw, and trembled, and ador'd.
But lest we call on rocks to hide,
A virgin Mother's at Thy side,[5]
    The pure in heart behold, and own love's gentle chord.

Oh, that this heart were cleans'd to see !
Go, earthly good, and leave me free,
    To see my God by sorrow torn,
In robes of rent humanity.[6]

[1] I believe in God.
[2] The Father Almighty, Maker of Heaven and earth.
[3] And in Jesus Christ, His only Son, our Lord.
[4] Who was conceived of the Holy Ghost.
[5] Born of the Virgin Mary.          [6] Suffered under Pontius Pilate.

And now before me that dread morn,—
And that pale form is bleeding borne,[1]
Of blending water and of blood
Flows forth the sacramental flood,[2]
And we without the tomb with Mary sit and mourn.[3]


E'en yet—disarming all our woe,
Thou goest down with us below![4]
   May we behold where Thou hast been,
And night of Thy dark burial know;—
   Thence see Thee by the moon serene;
   Rising behind th' Eternal screen,[5]
Now opening Heaven's ethereal bar,
And golden portals from afar,[6]
   On the right hand on high by dying Stephen seen.[7]


O mercy, with strange terrors blended!
Above, around, the skies are rended,
   Christ sits on high, and far and wide
Are hurrying Angels,—all is ended![8]
   Ah, hence with indolence and pride,
   With vain hope in the Crucified!—
In those dread truths do I believe?
Then let me not Thy presence grieve,
   But working in calm fear that fiery hour abide!


Spirit, foretelling and foretold,[9]
Lighting upon our Head of old,
   And thence through all His priesthood sent,
With power to loose, and power to hold;[10]
   Like oil on Aaron's head besprent,
   Till to his clothing's skirts it went:
Thence, to all time diffusing down,
Thou fill'st the Church from that blest crown
   With odorous graces sweet, o'erflowing and unspent.

---

[1] Was crucified.     [2] Dead.     [3] And buried.
[4] He descended into Hell.
[5] The third day He rose again from the dead.
[6] He ascended into Heaven.
[7] And sitteth on the right hand of God the Father Almighty.
[8] From whence He shall come to judge the quick and the dead.
[9] I believe in the Holy Ghost.    [10] The Holy Catholic Church.

Why mourn we left on earth alone?
When bound within that mystic zone [1]
   The dead and living are brought nigh,
And knit together all in one :
   O bond for mortal sense too high !
   And, pale Remorse, repress thy sigh ;
See the baptismal seal of Heaven,
The pledge of penitence forgiven ; [2]
   Go, sin no more, but learn a better strength to try !


Let me not mourn that stern decay
Is busy with this shed of clay,
   And wither'd leaves from off me fall ;—
I shall put on a fairer day
   Beyond my wintry funeral.—[3]
   O thought that doth the heart appal,
Bidding adieu to laggard time,
The unimagin'd steep to climb,
   With bars of night around, or Heaven's eternal hall ! [4]


## VII.

Thus rising, like a living mine,
From quarries of the Word divine,
The Apostolic symbol stands,
Moulded of old by saintly hands.
Within, o'ershadowing holy things,
Love stretches her cherubic wings.
Wind and rain they have no power,
To impair this heaven-built tower ;
Time, that beats down earthly things
With his "multitudinous wings,"
Serves but to strengthen and disclose
This temple in its dread repose.
Thus from a world of stern reproof,
   From storm and wind which fitful go,
   And shake each hope-built tower below,
We flee to an embowering roof,

[1] The Communion of Saints.    [2] The forgiveness of sins.
[3] The Resurrection of the body.    [4] And the life everlasting.

Thence see the shower—the shade—the sun,
O'er all without their courses run.
Oft 'mid the throng of spirits rude
We seem in friendless solitude,
And seek in vain some holding hand ;—
  But entering on that holy ground,
The veil is rais'd,—the mountains stand
  With fiery coursers girt, and fiery cars around.


### VIII.

Nor only in the holy shrine
The Faith holds forth this shield divine ;—
As with the traveller on his way,
Social or lonely, grave or gay,
The sky extends its circling bound,
The cloud-hung blue expanding round,—
Thus, wheresoe'er on earth we rove,
Its omnipresent form doth move,
Wherein the image of the skies,
And the eternal Gospel lies,
Infinity of strength and light,
And love e'en more than infinite.
  It is the breath of our new birth,
It is the light of our new morn,
Whence hues upon the soul are born,
  More durable than aught on earth.
When dawning life first let us in,
Into this house of grief and sin,
And Death stood by to mark his prey,—
Protectingly, our sheltering stay,
That Creed stood o'er the dangerous way—
An arch that open'd to the dome,[1]
The ancient Church's sacred home ;
An arch which, at Death's twilight bourne,
Lets out into the heavenly morn,[2]
And over-stretching the dread road,
Props on each side th' incumbent load,
Until the ransom'd have pass'd by,
In soberness most meet to bear the Judge's eye.

---

[1] In the Baptismal Service.       [2] In the Visitation of the Sick.

## IX.

Behold in Heaven yon glorious bow,
Which spans the gleaming world below !
The hues distinct in order glow,
Yet each in each doth melt unseen,
That none can mark the bound between:
Lo, such is Faith's mysterious scroll,
A multiform harmonious whole,
Together gather'd for our aid,
And in the darken'd heights displayed :
The Church shall ne'er that emblem want
Of her eternal covenant.
As on th' horizon's cloudy wall,
Where'er the golden sunbeams fall,
The colours in the rainbow found
Blend in a secret union bound.
E'en thus, where the true light hath shone,
The heart all truths shall hold, which rightly holdeth one.
    First Fear, which is the shadow true [1]
Of wrath divine to sinners due,
Looks out upon the deep, and tries
To sound her endless destinies ;—
That Fear with falling, falling wing,
Will to nought less than Godhead cling :
And he with eager heart and eyes
Who feeds on that dread sacrifice,
In aid Divine will seek to hide,
And on the living Word abide :
Feeling His presence, which doth bear,
And hold him buoyant in mid air.
O wondrous spell the heart to move,
And all her dark recesses prove !
    Lord, wake in me that holy awe,
Which through obedience learns Thy Law,
Till all my soul responsive own,
That Faith's mysterious union !

[1] Psalm xc. 11.

## X.

Yea, what is the Liturgic store
Of prayer and praise and sacred lore,
But changing notes as they proceed,
Unfolding all that wondrous Creed ;
Now rising to sublimer lays
In the Ambrosian song of praise,
Now calling pity from the skies
In penitential Litanies ?—
Or what the characters combin'd
In gifted holiness of mind,
But, in the secret spirit found,
The Creed contracting its vast bound ?
As all in one, earth, sea, and sky,
Are pictur'd in the gazing eye ;
Or some calm-bosom'd wave below
Mirrors the Sun's life-giving brow,
And holds, unbroken and entire,
The image of celestial fire ;
So may my heart reflective own
That Faith's all-perfect union !

## XI.

Shadows with us and phantoms dwell,
Nor can I now the vastness tell,
Wherein abides the Unchangeable.
    The things which mightiest seem'd erewhile,
The tree—the lake—the rustic pile—
Thro' memory's glass in childhood seen,
When manhood re-beholds, how mean,
Poor and contracted is the scene !
Then what will all things seem below,
When opes the heart our God to know ?
Fain would I learn heart-stilling awe,
While to that change I nearer draw ;
One who is doom'd to rove the main
Will gaze on that untravell'd plain,
Early and late will thither come,
Forgetful of his rural home,

And view th' expanse that boundless lies,
Form'd of the blending sea and skies.
  So would I gaze, ere I depart,
On that dread scene, and fill my heart,
Till gazing on reality,
All here shall shadows seem to me.
If freed from clouds of earthly care,
The soul becomes a mirror fair,
Where Truth from her empyreal shrines,
As in a secret palace shines,
Impregnating the crystal deeps,
Lightening the bed where darkness sleeps.
  If music of that calmer sphere
Find in the heart a mansion clear,
It with each virtue fills the soul,
And moulds to an harmonious whole ;
As runs the air the organ round,
And modulates the varied sound,—
Each pipe and stop in breathing gold
Answers with voices manifold.
  Nor marvel that, where'er it range,
Heaven's breath should work such wondrous change.
At Spring goes forth a viewless Power,
On leaf, on wing, on bird, on flower,
From buried Winter's winding-sheet
Wakening a sound or colour sweet,
Sky-tinctur'd plants, and feather'd things,
Fluttering upon melodious wings.
'Tis so with meaner sights of earth ;—
The light of our Baptismal birth,—
Shall it not turn each cross and care
Into some glorious form as fair,
Tho' eye and ear see nothing there?
  I know not much, I cannot tell,
I cannot see th' Invisible ;
But much I see for thoughtful praise ;
Tho' hedg'd with ill our mortal days,
The darker is the avenue,
More bright beyond Heaven's portal blue ;
And if a cloud should linger there,
'Tis passed—Heaven's gate again is fair.
If pride should lead to wanderings vain,

Remorse will oft restore ;—again
Awe-struck beneath that Creed we stand,
Its glories opening on each hand,
As vastness of the Heavens beyond
Bursts forth, struck by Night's ebon wand.


## XII.

Lord, who to set Thy pardon's seal,
To us thy Godhead dost reveal,
And on our skies the signal plant
Of the life-giving covenant :
Grant I may so obedience learn,
That I may thus those truths discern !
Grant I may so those truths discern,
That I may thus obedience learn !
Until their mutual benison
Disclose in me th' Eternal Son.
  So order me, *without Thy shrine,*
To walk in holy discipline,
Thy treasures in my soul to hide,
To steer me from the rocks of pride,
The lowliness of place to love,
And holiest truths by practice prove,
Resign'd, resolv'd, in meekness bold,
Thy steps to watch, Thy hand to hold,
That so Faith's scroll, which I repeat,
May find in me accordance meet.
  And teach me so, *Thy shrine within,*
Calm'd by Thy peace from worldly din,
The everlasting Faith to hear,
With fancy warm and spirit clear,
That, going thence, 'mid worldly strife
I daily wear a charmed life ;
That wisdom, like a living well,
Within my heart of hearts may dwell,
Strengthening and freshening, as we go,
The vale of sorrows here below !
Till Truth no more, in Nature's glass,
Shall like a shadow by us pass,
But we shall see her fountain bright,
And dwell with her in seas of light.

# The South Transept.

### The Epistle and Gospel.

[*Or Jesus Christ in History.*]

### I.

No more in mazes of the Psalmist's song,
    Is Christ disclos'd, as in a dim retreat ;
Nor sitting the prophetic shades among ;—
    But lighten'd by the living Paraclete
    The Church her children gathers 'neath His feet,
And shews anew upon each holier morn
    Tracks of His footsteps, or some lesson meet,
Words from th' Eternal roll, to cheer or warn,
And in a bracelet weaves her Sunday to adorn.

### II.

A few short Years make up our pilgrimage ;
    A few short Weeks make up the fleeting Year ;
Each Week doth bear a heavenly embassage ;
    With silent steps, as on a crystal stair,
    It comes and goes to Heaven.   With such sweet care
The Church hath deck'd each Week with blooming wings,
    Which else were earth's stern-hearted messenger
    Leading to Death ; she at perennial springs
Clothes it with holy light, and like an Angel brings.

## III.

The natural Year, swift shadow of the sun,
  Wakes from the earth a chequer'd tapestry,
To greet his footsteps as he passes on,
  Carpets of snow—sweet violets—lilies high—
  Then fields of waving gold—then varied dye
Of Autumn ; but the snow, and violets sweet,
  Lilies, and Autumn's wild variety,
And waving corn, fast as the sunbeams fleet,—
They bow their head and die beneath his hurrying feet.

## IV.

Not so the path the holy Church doth tread,
  The Year, that walketh in her light unseen,
Around its steps awakens from the dead
  Hopes that shall never die.   Through the serene
  Of the calm Sunday like an alley green,
Are seen th' eternal towers ; and where lights gild
  Death's twilight portal, us and them between,
She shews her suffering Lord ; throughout the wild,
Still shews her suffering Lord to her faint wandering child.

## V.

At every turn throughout Life's wilderness,
  In pillar'd fire, smote rock, or healed springs,
His presence she reveals, and power to bless :
  When the autumnal wind of ruin sings,
  She blends her Advent chaunt of happier things,
As louder swell the sounds of stern decay,
  The higher doth she lift her herald voice, till wings
And Angel forms are seen, and on our way
Springs from dark winter's womb the face of endless day—

### VI.

The Christmas dawn.   She thro' the waning night
 Her leaning child hath to that cradle led,
And bids him all unlearn but that meek sight
 And Heaven's own lesson, of the homely shed,
 The Babe and mother.   Nature now is dead,
And darksome; but in wintry skies is set
 A wreath that glitters o'er that Infant's head;
Her fairest stars are round His cradle met,
Like gems of light within His Kingly coronet,[1]—


### VII.

The Innocents, the Martyrs, and the one,
 For martyr's heart, and childlike innocence,
Belov'd and nearest.   Thus each duteous son
 She trains at His poor cradle, gaining thence
 Sermons of that diviner eloquence,
And as our sorrow's winters roll along,
 Brings to that childhood—in our manlier sense
Less have we ears for the angelic song,
Or heart to enter in with that meek shepherd throng.


### VIII.

Sweetly by mysteries are we wrapt around,
 Th' Epiphany's bright star is o'er the plain,
Mountain, and sea, where Jesus' steps are found,
 Coming to sojourn with the heirs of pain,
 And draw true hearts to Him with unseen chain.
Now she in sterner warnings points to where,
 In judgment and in glory He again,
Beyond the twilight of this silent air,
'Mid th' everlasting hills His chariot doth prepare.[2]

---

[1] The Saints' Days after Christmas Day.
[2] The last Sunday after the Epiphany refers to both the first and the
second Advent, as the Collect indicates.

## IX.

Then vernal Lent comes on—Nature puts up
    Her sweetest notes, and dons her fairest trim ;
The Church is drinking of her Saviour's cup,
    And far into the wild hath gone with him ;
    Nature's glad tones upon her prison dim
Break not, or with calm influence on the soul
    Come, like faint sounds of distant cherubim,
To cheer the chasten'd spirit, not control,
While prayer clears her dull eye to see th' eternal goal.

## X.

O thou, on Whom the Angels dare not gaze,
    In the deep bosom of Divinity,
But veil their faces from th' o'erpowering rays
    Of Thine eternal beauty ! Thee we see
    With countenance sore marr'd with agony
Beyond the sons of men.   O wondrous power
    Of Love divine ! shall man not watch with Thee
One little hour ! for scarce one fleeting hour
Set 'gainst the days of Heaven, is life's fast fading flower.

## XI.

A little further in the solemn grove,
    Into the bosom of the silent night,—
A little further onward let us move
    From the rude world—yet further—from the sight
    Of kindred and of friends, that so aright
We may discern our weakness, and apply
    Our hearts to God alone, while the broad light,
The witness of His sorrows, is on high,—
The paschal moon which o'er yon olive-mount stands by.

## XII.

Green Bethany, since that dread sorrow's blast,
   Thine olive-crown is turned all to sere—
Where from beneath thy feet is Cedron past?
   Where is the glorious temple standing near?
   But still the widow'd Church is lingering here.
Mary of Christ approv'd, and meekly wise,
   Teach her to bring with penitential fear
Some offering honour'd in thy Saviour's eyes,
The incense of the heart to embalm His obsequies.

## XIII.

Church of resign'd obedience! Rome may prize
   Her costlier garniture, and flaunting air;
Geneva boast her undress'd novelties;—
   Keep thou meek Mary's mien, divinely fair,
   Thy Saviour to approach with reverend care,
And lowly service—not where sounds aloud
   The voice that crieth in the streets, the stare
And gaze tumultuous of th' admiring crowd,
To stand beneath the cross with holy John allow'd.

## XIV.

Now, as the opening year doth gradual rise,
   Thro' toilsome months to her meridian tower,
Then full expands into her summer skies;
   Or plants that climb thro' many a wintry hour,
   And are unbosom'd in some fragrant flower:
Thus Whitsuntide, reveal'd in mighty flame,
   Opens from high Heaven's full mysterious dower,
And crowns the sacred year:—if without blame
The things which are divine with earthly I may name.

## XV.

And now her Lord is seen no more on earth,
   From the blest Three in One, withdrawn from view,
She showers down blessings of our better birth
   In falls of streaming light and pearly dew,
   Life-giving precepts, heavenly helps, and true
Unfading hopes : till all is eloquent
   Within this house roof'd o'er with crystal blue,
The earth, and sea, and glowing firmament,
Threefold one temple form, their Maker's holy tent.

## XVI.

Thus year by year the same her weekly strain,
   For not on turbulent seas of human pride,
But on the moveless rock she doth remain :
   Whate'er unquiet Creeds the earth divide,
   Between the Cherubims He doth abide,
Whose same still warning voice, afar and near,
   Is heard above the ever changeful tide :
Now as of old, unto a thousand year,[1]
Goes forth one weekly store—each willing heart and ear

## XVII.

One lesson learns.   Thus thro' advancing time
   Building His habitation from the ends
Of Earth and Heaven, of every tongue and clime,
   The dead and quick He in one temple blends,
   Wherein one prayer the Heavenly gate ascends.
Tho' Babel's curse rests on the world forlorn,
   And language, clime, and heart asunder rends,
Yet in th' unfailing Church, by age unworn,
Thy blessing still is fresh, thou Pentecostal morn !

[1] The Collects, Epistle, and Gospel can most of them be proved to have been in the Church more than twelve hundred years.   See "Palmer's Antiquities of the English Ritual."

## XVIII.

One soul, one tongue is there : th' Eternal Son,
  Her true Shechinah unreveal'd to sight,
Dwells in her living courts for ever One,
  Tho' manifold His gifts, and infinite
  The varied radiations of the light, -
While in His awful countenance we read :
  Withholding and imparting to our might,
And the requirements of our several need,
He quickens all the forms which from her breast proceed.


## XIX.

Her sacred Sundays, in their varied vest,
  And Saintly days, in colours of the skies,
With precept and with Prayer and warning drest,
  Were without Him but like th' enamell'd dyes
  On pictured panes, whose beauty hidden lies
All colourless, till from the veil of night
  The bright-hair'd Sun behind is seen to rise,
When lo, the holy Preachers spring to light,
Manifold shapes of life, in glowing vestures dight.


## XX.

And cloistral cells retir'd have caught the gleam,
  Thus each home-service hath His light enshrin'd ;
See on the bridal morn His radiance stream !
  Art thou a lonely one in lot and mind,
  Or hast thou earthly blessings but to find
That helplessness which on Earth's good relies ?
  Here is th' immortal Bridegroom, who doth bind
The virgin soul with more than bridal ties,
And hallows wedded love to holier charities.

## XXI.

Now at the couch of sickness would she stand,
  With that sweet lesson, like a lamp from high,
While Truth uplifts her awe-inspiring hand,
  Mercy with gentler accents would draw nigh,
" 'Twere good with Christ to suffer and to die ;"[1]
And when the soul, by sickness all unwound,
  O'er the expanse is shaken tremblingly,
She then discloses 'neath her girdle bound
A golden key, and cries, " I have a ransom found."[2]

## XXII.

Christ hath been in the waters, and the whole
  Of our baptismal being doth abound
With more of healing than Bethesda's pool,
  Stirr'd by the Angel, where there lay around
  The impotent, the maim'd, and sickness-bound ;
Emblem of this world's sorrows, 'mid the show
  Of portals fair, which over-arch the ground,
And seem to mock her children's varied woe.
Look on us, or we die where healing waters flow !

## XXIII.

From that baptismal well are onward cast
  The ancient paths, and fenc'd for evermore,
To the Eternal City ; on the past
  We think, and sigh, and our lost time deplore ;
  How have I fail'd to gain thy weekly lore,
Seed-time of heavenly harvests ! from a child
  Deep might my heart have treasur'd thy rich store
So transient scenes had ne'er my love beguil'd,
And left with empty hands, the soul with sin defil'd.

---

[1] See the Exhortation in the Visitation of the Sick.
[2] Job xxxiii. 24.

### XXIV.

But time remains for hope : each angry thought
    Against myself to turn, my bosom's pride,
And passionate complainings in me wrought
    Vent on myself; how have I wander'd wide;
    Woe is me, for the day will not abide;
Shadows of eve are stretched out, and we
    'Neath Night's dark wings our guilty heads would hide,
And steal to rest ; yet we can never be
As if we ne'er had been ;—but there the o'erwhelming sea

### XXV.

Shall burst from all its flood-gates, with the light
    Ushering the Judge's presence. Mother dear,
Oft as thy courts I enter, day or night,
    Thy voice is of forgiveness, full and clear,
    Hast thou no daily baptism ?—much I fear ;
Yet something o'er thine ancient threshold flings
    A dewy freshness ; where the fount stands near
Of our new birth-right, Hope reviving springs,
And o'er my fever'd brow soft waves her healing wings.

### XXVI.

Church of my country, unto thee is lent
    More than e'en Nature hath in ways of love ;
A vine, that spreads abroad a living tent
    Of shelter, shade, and food,—a rocky cove,—
    The eye maternal of the gentle dove,—
The swan's soft wing spread o'er her snowy throng,—
    The gaze of the stern eagle fix'd above,—
The doe's retiring step, that with her young
Bounds from the gazer's eye the branching woods among.

## XXVII.

The archers sore have griev'd thee ;—wilt thou flee,
   And leave us? so hereafter, hither bent,
Some pensive traveller may return, and see
   All that remains, a mantle rudely rent,
   Or weep beside a mouldering monument.
I saw an aged pile,[1] calm in decay,
   Which, where the Wye his mountain windings went,
Look'd from its ivy mantle, stern and grey,
While little birds sang thro' their summer holiday ;


## XXVIII.

The sheep were browsing in the sacred hall,
   Which once had echoed to the choral song ;
And that old wandering river seem'd to call
   On ancient memories ; and the mountain throng
   Stood by in solemn consciousness ; among
Rent walls the wild flowers hung, thro' blended view
   Of arches and tall piles, in ruin strong
And beautiful, shone the celestial blue,
And there with a black cloud the Sun contending through.


## XXIX.

Thoughts of our Church like moon-beams seem'd to peer,
   And made the desolation more forlorn ;
It was an hour for contemplation's tear :
   But 'tis not ours o'er ruin'd wrecks to mourn,
   For thro' the broken rents, which Time hath worn,
Shines our celestial House ; our Father blest
   Should teach us thus how vain each earthly bourne,
Though fairest seeming, holiest, and best ;—
The more to seek for nought but His eternal rest.

[1] Tintern Abbey.

## 𝕿𝔥𝔢 𝔒𝔯𝔞𝔱𝔬𝔯𝔦𝔢𝔰.

*Consolations and Strongholds.*

---

## FESTIVALS.

SPHER'D in its orb, each radiant Festival
    Upon our annual path in turn appears,
And, like the lights on the ethereal wall,
    Each its new shade of varying lustre wears,—

Each its new thought, new lesson, till at length
    The combinations of their brightness blend
To form the wreath of Truth, Light's gather'd strength
    The knowledge of our God, our being's end.

One while the Infant Martyrs throw their mild
    And gentle radiance upon childhood's grave ;
Which some sad mother hath of grief beguil'd,
    Sooth'd with the pledge of the fresh saving wave.

Not so when glorious Michael stands confest,
    With ministering hosts and bright array,
Faith sees around her many an Angel guest,
    Like stars, forgotten in the glare of day.

Not so when Saints of God around us come,
    Till half unmindful of ourselves forlorn,
Of th' intervening veil and silent tomb,
    We tread with them the courts of heavenly morn.

Now holy Matthew calls, for Jesus' sake,
    " Beware of Mammon and the treacherous leaven,"
Leaving the gainful Galilean lake,
    Calls us with him to barter Earth for Heaven.

Now John, whose ravish'd glance is fix'd above,
  Drinking the beams which from the Godhead stream,
Puts on the calmness of Angelic love,
  While life beneath him seems a fleeting dream.


Thus from the sphere in which it lay conceal'd
  As thro' its zodiac rolls the Sacred Year,
Some grace is ever and anon reveal'd,
  To duteous hearts fresh influence to bear.


Nor deem it profitless, on chosen days
  The ever-busy soul to discipline
To clothe herself with robes of holy praise,
  Of countless hues as in the sunbeam shine.


As sunbright days transform the teeming grain,
  So these do mould the temper, till it grows
To full and golden ripeness, with the train
  Of Sabbath thoughts unask'd, and Christ's repose.


As when on Sunday morn insensate things
  With the glad spirit sweetly harmonize,
Till leafy woods, and beasts, and flowing springs,
  Seem but to join heard music in the skies :—


The mind clothes all with light from her own store,
  And over mute creation spreads her wings ;
Then on those wings to Nature's God to soar,
  On sympathies of earth she heavenward springs :—


So these lift up the soul to happier lands,
  To hear what strains to the Redeem'd belong ;
Many the gate where Sion's daughter stands,
  And at each portal sings a new-made song.

### THE NICENE CREED.

August Consistory, in whose dread pale
  Together comes assembled Christendom ;
While Kings, the nursing-fathers, watch the scale !

  They come, faint image of the general doom,
From the four winds of Heaven, and with them meet
  The spirits of their fathers from the tomb,—

Call'd by the witness-bearing Paraclete
  To testify to wandering Israel.—
But who is set on Sion's judgment-seat ?

  'Tis One too glorious to be visible
To mortal eyes, but Who unto the end
  Dwells in His Church—the true Emmanuel.

He from the heights of Heaven deigns to descend,
  And takes His seat on David's ancient throne ;
And, where Christ is, th' Angelic hosts attend.

  He, 'mid the golden candlesticks alone
Walks, and attemper'd to divine accord
  The assembled multitude His presence own.

Lo ! in His voice is heard th' unfailing Word,
  Like sound of many waters ; and again
There goeth from His mouth a two-edg'd sword.

  He high enthron'd above dark Error's reign,
With His Apostles round His sacred feet,
  Shall yesterday, to-day, and aye remain.

Then wonder not that where her children meet,
  The Church but gathers up her ancient lays,
And fuller diapason doth repeat.

Thus in earth's distant mines are hid the rays,
Which light the breast-plate in Truth's living zone,
   Bearing the voice of God to latest days ;—

Strings brought together of responsive tone,
   Which form a harp by Wisdom's holy spell,
From which proceeds the Church's orison ;—

Stones wrought by unseen hands, and moulded well,
Which, knit together, build a mystic shrine,
   Wherein resides a living oracle ;—

And when it goeth forth,—Earth's furthest line,
   And echo answers from the distant skies,
Acknowledging the voice of Truth divine.

Here in our solemn Minster it doth rise
Like some ancestral pillar to behold,[1]
   The witness-stone inscrib'd with living eyes ;

With sculptur'd tablets on each side enroll'd,
   Writ by the finger of th' Eternal Son,—
The universal Faith which was of old.

Rest not without to gaze, but pass still on,
And thou shalt find within a sacred cell,
   A holy Altar, and a cross thereon,

Faith's oratory, and calm citadel,
   Angelic haunts, the house of benison,
Where thou mayst grateful pray, and ever dwell.

---

[1] "This Council in Nicæa," says Athanasius, "is truly a pillar set up with an inscribed warning against every kind of heresy."—Ep. ad Afros. l. c. 899, quoted by Keble, Sermon on Tradition, p. 126, 3rd Ed.

## THE BLESSING.

### I.

As Simeon for his last release,—
As crowds when evening shades increase
Till Jesus bids them go in peace : [1]

As thirsty lands to summer skies,
The maiden on her mistress' eyes,
As travellers for the morning's rise :

Thus, heavenward turn'd her listening ear
Faith waits her Saviour's peace to hear,
In words of His own messenger.

### II.

For vapours sent on wings of Even,
From pining earth to pitying Heaven,
The freshening dew to her is given.

The drop, which through the ocean strays,
Touch'd by the Sun's pure Indian rays
Becomes a pearl of living blaze.

So for our earthly sacrifice
Of prayer and praise, returning thrice
The blessing of celestial price :—

---

[1] Our Saviour's *dismissing* the crowd is often alluded to, as if it were
accompanied with some significant action : thus St Matt. xiv. 22, "while
He *dismissed*," and 23, when He "had *dismissed*" them.

## III.

More than the dying patriarch knew,
Who o'er his sons his mantle threw,—
Words which Christ's dying gift renew.

Not such the spreading incense cloud ;
Not such the music thrilling loud ;
Nor Aaron's voice o'er silent crowd.[1]

Shield of the Spirit, saving spell,
Faith's amulet invisible,
Ever about us come and dwell.

[1] Ecclus. l. 16, 20.

## DISTANT CHURCH BELLS.

Up steeps reclining in th' Autumnal calm,
The woodland nook retir'd, and quiet field,
　　Upon the tranquil noon
　　The Sunday chime is borne;

Rising and sinking on the silent air,
With many a dying fall most musical,
　　And fitful bird hard by
　　Blending harmoniously.

The moon is looking on the sunny earth;
The little fleecy cloud stands still in Heaven,
　　Making the blue expanse
　　More still and beautiful.

If aught there be upon this rude bad earth,
Which Angels from their happy spheres above
　　Could lean and listen to,
　　It were those peaceful sounds.

There is unearthly balm upon the air,
And holier lights which are with Sunday born,
　　That man may lay aside
　　Himself, and be at rest.

The week-day cares, like shackles, from us fall,
As from our Lord the clothings of the grave;
　　And we too seem with Him
　　To walk in endless morn.

Not that these musical wings would bear us up
On buoyant thoughts too high for sinful man,
　　But that they speak the best
　　Which earth hath left to give,

Of better hopes, and prayer, and penitence,
Rising in incense on the sacred air
　　From many a woodland spire,
　　Or hill-embosom'd tower;

That sadness, and privation, and earth's loss
In the great sea of goodness are forgot,
      And sense of stern decay
      Is lost in sweet repose.

So deep are all things stamp'd with vanity,
So fading, and so fleeting, and so frail,—
      And we too, while we speak,
      Dropping ourselves away,—

That envy, and unkindness, and revenge,
In very pity for themselves might weep,
      Coping with a poor shade,
      With real sad unrest.

It may be that our hopes may be deceived,
And we found wanting ; yet a little while
      We 'gainst ourselves will hope,
      And against hope rejoice.

For earth hath nothing else found worth our care,
And if we lose her all, we nothing lose,
      So poor while it remain'd,
      And so short-liv'd when gone !

But if we are beguil'd by her false charms,
By her enthralling ways and prospects fair,
      Her promises of good
      The shadow of a shade,

Fleeting behind to-morrow—on—and on—
If we, by her vain impotence beguil'd,
      Lose our great being's end—
      We are beguil'd indeed !

## The Sepulchral Recesses.

### The Churchman's Friends.

---

#### HERBERT.

[George Herbert (1593-1632), Rector of Bemerton.   His " Country
Parson " consists of rules drawn up for the regulation of his own
conduct.]

MEEK Herbert, ere of thee I sing,
   'Tis thou must lend the string,
On Jesus' breast thou art asleep,
   Or thou wouldst wake and weep,
That any one should sing of thee
   Laid in thy poverty.

But all our Church doth bear along
   The echoes of thy song,
Thy Country Pastor sweet and stern
   Her children fain would learn ;
Then let the light that fills her shrine
   On thy meek urn recline.

For now thou art a holy thing,
   And singing the great King
For ever with a nobler strain ;
   Nor praise of ours can pain,
If we be tuned by thy lays
   To sing thy " Master's " praise.

Meek Herbert, would that such as I
   Could learn thy lesson high,
Those ways that made thy spirit's tone
   A midnight orison,[1]
Thy more than manly wisdom free,
   And child's simplicity.

---

[1] See an anecdote in Walton's Life of Herbert, p. 83, Oxford edit.,
1805.   "His answer was, that the thought of what he had done would
prove music to him at midnight."

For Angels ever with thee are,
   And, in their presence fair,
Thy spirit feels it poor and mean,
   But golden thoughts doth glean
Which fall like light from off their wings,
   When bow'd to earth it sings.

## BUTLER.

[Joseph Butler (1692-1752), Bishop of Durham. The central thought of this sonnet is the deep sense of the Order of the Universe, which was constantly present to the great philosopher's mind, and which found expression in his dying words.]

I SAW within a glass vast worlds of light,
   Launch'd multitudinous on the shoreless sea,
   While, far outspread, the boundless Deity
Sat brooding 'mid the peopled Infinite.
Within her and around her the dark sprite
   Sees—but to know she sees not—the vast zone,
   All bodiless, hung from th' Eternal's throne,
And hears strange melodies on th' ear of night.
   Thus on my heart of hearts still silently
   Lingers the echo of thy solemn strain,
Thoughtful and saintly Butler ! then above,
   Dark clouds between, is seen a golden chain,
   And earth and Heaven breathe with Divinity;—
I walk with holy trembling and deep love.

# KING GEORGE III.

[The poet numbers this king among the English saints in the con-
viction that it was his piety which preserved the Church and nation
from the horrors of the French Revolution.]

AND thee, of firm-set foot, and stern advance,
  Giv'n to whose prayers she haply yet doth stand
  To hold Truth's lamp unto a thankless land,
Our Church shall own.   For no unholy chance,
Nor strength of counsel, nor embattled lance,
  Nor princely league, nor sea-victorious band,
  Shielded her from the pestilential brand,
And fiery breath of parricidal France :
  But one who drank at her diurnal source,
One who his anchor had within the veil.
Hers was the breath that fill'd his regal sail
  Right onward, Hers the star that led his course
  Thro' the tempestuous skies ; that, 'mid wild force,
Disloyal tongues, fall'n kings, hearts faint and frail,
All look'd to him, in Her calm firmness free,
Sacredly wise in mild simplicity.

## WILSON.

[(1663-1755) Bishop of Sodor and Man. The reference at the end of the sonnet is to the restoration of primitive customs in his diocese, so that Lord Chancellor King said that the ancient discipline of the Church was found in all its purity in the Isle of Man. The island was converted to Christianity by St Patrick about A.D. 440.]

MONA, may Ocean's waves that gird thee round
Keep watch about thy shores, as holy ground,
And lift their suppliant hands, nor plead in vain,
And thine Apostle's See e'en yet remain !
For, louder than those waves thy rocks among,
That saintly name once had a thrilling tongue,[1]
Which pleaded for thy sea-encircled strand ;
And still doth plead.   Woe worth the reckless hand
That shall remove thy landmark, and defile
His living monument, thou sacred Isle.
He needeth nought of us, true-hearted saint,
Nor storied stone, nor monumental plaint,
But much we need of him, while in his praise
Shall the memorial live of pure primeval days.

---

[1] Cardinal Fleury obtained an order that no French privateer should be allowed to ravage the island, on Bishop Wilson's account.

## ANDREWES.

[1555-1626. The greatest bishop of Winchester since the Reformation, eminent not only as prelate, but as a preacher and writer. The reference in the first stanza is to his attitude on his beautiful monument in St Saviour's, Southwark. That in the second is to his "Devotions."]

STILL praying in thy sleep,
  With lifted hands and face supine !
Meet attitude of calm and reverence deep,
  Keeping thy marble watch in hallow'd shrine.

  Thus, in thy Church's need,
    Enshrin'd in ancient Liturgies,
Thy spirit shall keep watch and with us plead,
  While from our secret cells thy prayers arise.

  Still downward to decay
    Our Church is hast'ning more and more ;
But what else need we but with thee to pray
  That God may yet her treasures lost restore ?[1]

[The following, by Keble, appeared in the earlier editions instead of the above:—

### HOOKER.

  Voice of the wise of old !
  Go breathe thy thrilling whispers now
In cells where learned eyes late vigils hold,
  And teach proud Science where to veil her brow.

  Voice of the meekest man !
  Now, while the Church for combat arms,
Calmly do thou confirm her awful ban,
  Thy words to her be conquering, soothing charms.

  Voice of the fearless saint !
  Ring like a trump, where gentle hearts
Beat high for Truth, but, doubting, cower and faint :—
  Tell them, the hour is come, and they must take their parts.]

[1] " That what is wanting in her may be supplied,
  "that what remains in her may be strengthened."
                    BP. ANDREWES' DEVOTIONS.

# The South Porch.

### *The Church in Fear.*

EDEN was in her morning beauty rife,
Opening her bosom, like some vernal flower,
When crept the deadly serpent from his bower
    To poison all the founts of life.

Men smil'd at one that wrought a house of wood,—
Married and gave in marriage—built and made
Foundations; when the sky was overlaid,
    And open'd, came the rushing flood.

Sodom in pamper'd pride was revelling,
And Jordan in the sunshine basking nigh,—
The thunder-arm was hid in the blue sky,—
    'Neath flowers the sulphurous whirlwind's wing.

Not when King David cried, My son, My son!
But when before him, on his throne reclin'd,
Wav'd number'd hosts, like trees before the wind,—
    Look forth, the plague is now begun!

Not when sick Hezekiah hid his brow,
But when he, glorying, shew'd his treasur'd pride,
'Twas then the Angel took the veil aside,—
    Lo, Babylon, and chains, and woe!

The Babylonian, 'mid the heavenly stars
Walk'd in his glory;—when the sky was riven,
Fell, like the thunder-bolt, the voice from Heaven,
    And the dark cloud his vision mars.

The Eastern Queen of cities sat in state,
Throwing unwonted lustre on night's hall;—
Behold, the fiery hand is on the wall,
    The Mede is knocking at the gate.

When Tyre with jewels deck'd her sea-born nest,
Sitting in beauty 'mid her watery flock,
The nations heard her cry;—upon the rock
    The lonely sea-bird sits to rest.


Not when Christ's flock were wand'ring, earth-disown'd,
But when on her seven hills, attir'd in gold,
Sat Babylon, 'mid sorceries manifold,—
    'Twas then the poison'd cup went round.


At the vex'd Church's feet, oppress'd and wrong'd,
When Constantine laid down the imperial pride,
Her gate once narrow she unfolded wide,
    And the mix'd world her temple throng'd.


When Liberty her triumph loudest rais'd,
And on the popular billow William sail'd
Into our thrones, Britain the stranger hail'd,—
    The Church look'd on, and blindly gaz'd.


Then her best sons were from the vineyard cast,
While loyal Truth in secret sat to mourn,
She knew not, of her strength and glory shorn,
    The leav'n to her deep bosom past.


Since then, her children flock to Freedom's shrine;
She hath forgot her sackcloth, seeming fair,
Her discipline, her penitence, and prayer;
    And wakes all nerveless to restrain.


When she hath hid her Cross, with glad accord
The world will welcome her, in beauty shrin'd,
And woo her charities, and, seeming kind,
    Stretch forth those hands that slew her Lord.


Yea, often will she stop her gilded car,
To hear of treasures op'd by pardon free,
And fadeless joys, and calm eternity,—
    Then passion-borne hurry afar.

Thus as her voice shall higher rise and higher,
The Priests of God disown'd, His Word put by,
Then shall the stars shake on the trembling sky,
And forth shall break the Judgment-fire.

# PART III

# The Choir.

## The Steps to the Choir

*The Litany.*

### I.

Ye Litanies of ancient prayer,
　　Here, in our holy ground,
Ye rise a bright and crystal stair,
　　Which clouds and gloom surround ;
A crystal stair the purer Heavens ascending,
Fair as the seas and skies, at evening's portal blending.

### II.

Fair as when, from yon western door,
　　The showering sunbeams stream,
And restless motes, which sink and soar,
　　Shine in the silver gleam ;
Thus shapes of human woe within that shrine,
Come forth, and catch the light, mingling with hope divine.

### III.

It is a stair which climbs a throne,
　　Within a sacred tower,
The tower of truth to man made known,—
　　Mysterious love and power ;
The soul-sustaining truth, of One in Three,
And Three in One, enthron'd o'er the tumultuous sea.[1]

### IV.

It is a stair descending low,
　　'Mid shapes of mortal ill,
Into the deeps of sin and woe,
　　Deeps opening deeper still,
Till an upholding hand is stretch'd to raise
From the unfathom'd gulf of sin-deluding ways.[2]

[1] The Invocation.　　　[2] The Deprecations.

### V.

It is a stair where, evermore,
 The Church's duteous feet,
On mysteries of Christian lore
 Ascend the Mercy-seat;
Brought near in Christ, she dares to intercede,
And, in His robe arrayed, for fallen man to plead.[1]

### VI.

It is a stair by Love allow'd,
 Where Heaven-born Prayers may pass;
As when the sun looks on a cloud,
 When suddenly the mass
Turns to a wondrous arch and glorious way,
Built for Heaven's messengers by the emerging ray.

### VII.

Descending here with sky-lit lamp,
 They enter palaces,[2]
Or cells of sorrow, dark and damp,
 With voice of sweet release,
Now break the prison bars with gentle might,
Now ope on sinful hearts kind mercy's cheering light.

### VIII.

There Prayers may pass;—I deem them not,
 As heathen poets told,[3]
Forgetting man by man forgot,
 Half-sighted, lame, and old,
Following fleet-footed Ate round the earth
To heal the woes she makes, not antedate their birth:

---

[1] The Obsecrations.  [2] The Intercessions for the King, &c.
    [3] See Homer, b. ix. 498.

## IX.

But rather bright-hair'd Angel guests,
    Fair children of the skies,—
And sure and swift on kind behests,
    And healing embassies,
Quick as the light to th' Heaven of Heavens ye spring,
Then shake celestial air from your returning wing.


## X.

Thus when of old, beneath the skies,
    Or holier aisles around,
The Church her moving Litanies
    Like incense had unbound,
Away had Pestilence and Famine fled,
And Heresy had hid her bad embolden'd head.


## XI.

And now where is her arm of strength,
    When all th' unchristian rout
Are gather'd, and are set at length
    Her Israel's camp about?
'Tis not in sword, or banded multitude,
But in the hidden lamps, with heavenly oil endued.


## XII.

Invok'd by David's son of old,
    Thy Presence rose to sight;
In courts of cedar and of gold
    Was shed the Living Light;
One more than David's son for us hath prayed,
Whose viewless presence fills His Church's mystic shade.

## The Approach to the Choir.

### *Despondency.*

AND is this all? and what avail
　　These cloistral watchings pale?
And what to walk in holy heed
　　Beneath the o'erarching Creed?
Or track Heaven-lighten'd caves of thought,
　　In prayer which Jesus taught?
These to His presence-chamber bring,
　　Where, as an abject thing,
In that true light for evermore
　　We should ourselves deplore.

### *Invitation.*

O DROOPING Sadness, whose rapt gaze
　　Hath been on face of slow-pac'd night
　　Watching the beam of dawning light,
Come here, and learn thy song of praise.

O Singleness of eye and heart,
　　Which fleetest over earthly things,
　　Nor fold'st below thy weary wings,
Here find thy rest, and take thy part.

O sacred Awe, whose downcast look
　　Is on the pavement of the shrine,
　　Which all unearthly seems to shine,
Look up, a healing Presence brook!

## The Skreen.

*Disciplina Arcani.*

NATURE withdraws from human sight
  The treasures of her light;
In earth's deep mines, or ocean's cells,
  Her secret glory dwells.
'Tis darkly thro' Night's veil on high
  She shews the starry sky
And where of beauty aught is found,
  She draws a shade around;
Nor fully e'er unveils to sense
  Steps of bright Providence.

When out of Sion God appear'd
  For perfect beauty fear'd,
The darkness was His chariot,
  And clouds were all about.
Hiding His dread sublimity,
  When Jesus walked nigh,
He threw around His works of good
  A holier solitude;
Ris'n from the grave appear'd to view
  But to a faithful few.

Alone e'en now, as then of old,
  The pure of heart behold
The soul-restoring miracles
  Wherein His mercy dwells;
New marvels unto them reveal'd,
  But from the world conceal'd.
Then pause, and fear,—when thus allow'd
  We enter the dark cloud,
Lord, keep our hearts, that soul and eye
  Unharm'd may Thee descry.

Who shall ascend into the hill of the Lord? or who shall stand in His holy place?

# The Choir.

## THE SACRAMENTAL HYMN.

He that hath clean hands, and a pure heart.—PSALM xxiv. 3, 4.

## ℭhe ℭhoir.

*The Sacramental Hymn.*

### I. 1.

*Men.*

GLORY be to God on high :
 Beyond where dwells the evening star
 In his golden house afar ;
 Where upon th' eternal noon
 Never look'd the silver moon ;
 Thro' innumerable skies
 Multitudinous voices rise,
And in harmonious concord meet,
 Around our Saviour's feet,
Beneath mysterious veils descending from His seat.

### 2.

*Angels.*

Peace be upon earth below :
 God is in His holy hill ;
 Let the earth and sea be still ;
 And the child of sin and woe
 Come before Him, bowing low ;
 In his breast the living One
 Makes His altar and His throne ;
He comes from Heaven's high citadel,
 With men on earth to dwell,—
The pure in heart alone shall see th' Invisible.

### 3.

*Men and Angels.*

Good will to man from God above :
 From dwellings of th' Eternal Word,
 Whose house is immortality,
 He letteth down the triple cord,
 Of Faith and Hope and Love from high ;
 And from His cradle to His throne
 Extends a living zone,
Which binds anew the ancient heavens and earth,
Now teeming with the throes of a more glorious birth.

### II. 1.

#### *Men.*

Glory be to God on high :
  Angel faces stand aloof
  On the starry temple roof,—
  Your bright-wing'd consistory
  Round our altars we deem nigh ;
  Now, in awe and dread amaze,
  From your crystal heights ye gaze ;
And see the sun that lights you, sent
    From your deep firmament,
And coming down with man to make his lowly tent.

### 2.

#### *Angels.*

Peace be upon earth below :
  Wisdom deep in sacred lore
  Hides within her secret store,
  Like the sweet soul of the lyre,
  Slumbering in the silent wire ;
  But in Christ their blending tone,
    In responsive union,
  Rings out with solemn harmonies,
    The music of the skies,
At whose heart-soothing sound the evil spirit flies.

### 3.

#### *Men and Angels.*

Good will to man from God above :
  The Law and Prophets here have won
    The glory of their Master's light,
  As Moses and Elias shone
    With Him upon the mountain height :
  The Gospel in His light display'd,
    Is all translucent made,
As when, reveal'd on Tabor's holy ground,
With light divinely burn'd His clothing's skirt around.

### III. 1.

#### *Men.*

Glory be to God on high,
   Where, in bosom of all space,
   Sun and moon have found no place,
   Where lies the waveless, shoreless sea
   Of eternal clarity ;
   Where the Saints have fled life's woes
   To their haven of repose,
And earth beneath them as they soar,
   Releas'd for evermore,
Seems but a wither'd leaf on some bright wat'ry floor.

### 2.

#### *Angels.*

Peace be upon earth below :
   Pride and envy have no place
   Where His sons God doth embrace ;
   Where the fountain overflows,
   Whose full breast no lessening knows ;
   Where old Eden's fallen towers
   The new tree of life embowers,
That, fearless of the fiery brand,
   And bold in God's command,
There man may eat, and live, led by Angelic hand.

### 3.

#### *Men and Angels.*

Good will to man from God above :
   Here at His feast doth Love preside,
   Love weaves anew the nuptial tie,
   Love decks with health the living Bride,
   And clothes with holy poverty :
   The ancient Heavens, array'd in might,
   Walk their high paths of light,
As Duty marshals their appointed way,
But Love attunes their steps to an harmonious lay.

## IV. 1.

### *Men.*

Glory be to God on high,
　Where the armies of the skies
　Stand in snowy galaxies,
　Fair as dreams, in bright platoon,
　Brighter than th' Autumnal moon,
　Where many a wild avenue
　Draws afar the eager view ;
　And worlds, in darker distance sown,
　　People the living zone,
Like sparks that issue forth from Glory's burning throne.


## 2.

### *Angels.*

Peace be upon earth below,
　Where in visions half divine
　Sunsets part, and parting twine
　Bridal robes of earth and sky,
　Passing fair, tho' born to die ;
　Where unearthly hues adorn
　The advance of rising morn ;
　And dimly thro' the gates of earth,
　　'Mid want, decay, and dearth,
There wander embryo shapes which speak a heavenly birth.


## 3.

### *Men and Angels.*

Good will to man from God above :
　A little while I hid my face ;
　　But Mercy shall to thee abound,
　Firm as the mountains in their place,
　　With everlasting arms around :
　Yea, the strong mountains' firm array,
　　And hills, shall pass away,
But in that hour my Love shall stand with thee,
Rising from mists of Time, a mansion strong and free.

## V. 1.

### Men.

Glory be to God on high :
  Bright and golden panoplies,
  Sweet Angelic harmonies,
  That, all dark to our weak sight,
  In the centre of all light,
  Sing, and singing sweetly move,—
'Tween you and the fount of Love,
There never yet came aught of blame,
    But, free from sin and shame
Fresh in your innocence ye lift your glad acclaim.


### 2.

### Angels.

Peace be upon earth below,
  Where Repentance, lowly-wise,
  In spirit of self-sacrifice,
  Lowly bows her shame to feel,
  And her sin-wrought wounds to heal ;
  Till the breath of new desires,
  Here enkindling holy fires,
Devours the seeds of death and sin,
    Until there stirs within
A voice not all unmeet His praises to begin.


### 3.

### Men and Angels.

Good will to man from God above :
  Here encircling round him swells
    The sea of boundless charity,
  Which thence doth work thro' secret cells,
    Unnumber'd fountains to supply,
  Till through Creation's utmost round
    Sweet flowing streams abound,
Upon whose banks His creatures find repose,
Where many a flower lies hid, or towering cedar grows.

## VI. 1.

*Men.*

Glory be to God on high,
　　Where the lov'd and lost ones meet
　　Safe beneath their Saviour's feet :
　　Faces dear, 'tis now ye smile,
　　Ye, whom I have miss'd awhile,
　　Missing you, I long have hung
　　Downcast, silent, and unstrung,
　And faint and feeble is the strain
　　　I e'er shall wake again,
Until I join your lays beyond the reach of pain.

## 2.

*Angels.*

Peace be upon earth below ;
　　Seek ye, mourners, for release ?
　　Here behold the cup of peace !
　　Here, with your poor fleshly ties,
　　Are divinest sympathies ;
　　Tho' hid a little while from sight
　　These spirits soft that cheer'd your night,
　They are but gone like stars of morn,
　　　Before the sun is born ;—
Still near you tho' unseen His temple they adorn.

## 3.

*Men and Angels.*

Good will to man from God above :
　　Tho' death doth raise his veil between,
　　　Yet Thee in them, and them in Thee,
　　We solemnize awhile unseen,
　　　And soon the cleansed sight shall see.
　　The Church dwells here a sufferer still,
　　　Yet, born of heavenly birth,
　Her nurture is of heavenly food, until
Her stature fills the sky, while she doth walk on earth.

## VII. 1.

*Men.*

Glory be to God on high :
Where is Death, that uncouth thing ?
  He hath now a sheltering wing.
  Awful phantom, where art thou ?
  Heaven's own bloom is on thy brow,
  Earth hath nothing half so fair,
  Christ's own flesh and blood is there.
On thy cold lips and silent tongue
  A deathless health hath sprung,
Which thro' the days of Heaven for ever shall grow young.


### 2.

*Angels.*

Peace be upon earth below.
  Shape of woe ! if form that be
  Which is but deformity,
  Death, the gloomy King of tears,
  Waited on by spectral fears,
  Now thy dark-illumin'd shade
  Is in hope a solemn glade,
That leadeth to the place of God.
  Christ is the staff and rod ;
His Presence lights the vale which He Himself hath trod.


### 3.

*Men and Angels.*

Good will to man from God above :
  The light breaks forth on shapes afar
    That darkly throng'd life's closing gate,
  And there keeps watch a gleaming star,
    Where dismal shadows seem'd to wait ;
  As clouds along the bending sky,
    Like mountains pil'd on high,
  When lo, Thy gentle gale Thou bidd'st to blow,
And into empty air before Thy breath they go.

## VIII. 1.

*Men.*

Glory be to God on high :
  God hath risen and bent His bow,
  Lo, before His face they go,
  Discontent with fretting chain,
  Sin and sorrow, shame and pain,
  To night's jail they troop away,
  Like mists before the rising ray,
Which long hath climb'd conceal'd from sight,
    Then from some mountain height
Majestically breaks upon the rear of night.

## 2.

*Angels.*

Peace be upon earth below :
  Here there is a living cup—
  Wells of water springing up
  Unto life that cannot die,—
  The pledge of immortality ;
  'Tis a fount of heavenly strength,—
  A sea of love with breadth and length
Proportion'd to th' undying soul,—
    The spirit of controul
Which takes the reins of thought, and urges to the goal.

## 3.

*Men and Angels.*

Good will to man from God above :
  The bending Heavens have brought Him down,
    From out their heights of highest height,
  The exil'd wanderer to own ;
    The abysses of the Infinite
  Are all about Him,—seas and sky
    Of glory,—ear and eye
Cannot discern, nor speak the mortal tongue,
But in the heart's deep home the Spirit hath a song.

## IX. 1.

### *Men.*

Glory be to God on high.
    Scarcely, earth's new cradle round,
    Had ye raised your gladsome sound,
    When Creation drooping hung,
    And your alter'd descant rung :
    Then to pleading Mercy given,
    Drops of pardon fell from Heaven,
The thorn of sorrow bore the rose,
    Balm was in woman's throes,
And the dark gates of death the Lord of Life disclose.

### 2.

### *Angels.*

Peace be upon earth below.
    Nature smooth'd her mournful brow,
    When she saw the gleaming bow,
    Which encompass'd the dark place
    With the covenant of grace :
    Oft as down Heaven's cloudy stair
    Comes that harbinger so fair,
Glad Earth with incense-breathing dew,
    Her veil of sorrow through,
Looks tearfully to Heaven, and grateful smiles anew.

### 3.

### *Men and Angels.*

Good will to man from God above.
    As, o'er the flood-reviving earth
      That witness stands in Heaven secure,
    Thus o'er our new and better birth
      This Sacramental seal is sure :
    Until the sun shall make his bed,
      And Time be withered,
The pledge of saving mercy shall remain ;
None to His breast shall turn, and thither turn in vain.[1]

    [1] Isaiah liv. 9, 10.

## X. 1.

*Men.*

Glory be to God on high.
　　When his people He would save,
　　Seas hung back on wondering wave,
　　And beheld their Master nigh,
　　Marshalling their deeps on high ;
　　Then beneath the watery wall
　　Banner'd hosts went at His call,
And safe were harbour'd, till again,
　　　Fresh bursting from his chain,
With tumbling billows rush'd the bold avenging Main.

### 2.

*Angels.*

Peace be upon earth below,
　　Which life's toils but rock to rest,
　　Cradled on a Father's breast.
　　When the ark descended low
　　Jordan's streams forgot to flow,
　　Bridling back their horned march
　　To a hanging wavy arch,
And, lo, upon the promis'd strand,
　　　There stood an armed Hand,
No sword of yours doth gain this fair and flowery land.

### 3.

*Men and Angels.*

Good will to man from God above.
　　Lo, in the shadowy vale of years,
　　　Oft imag'd in redeeming love,
　　'Tis Christ the living Way appears,
　　　And leads to happier coasts above :—
　　Ready to whelm on either hand,
　　　The awe-struck waters stand,
And, with their ancient brethren of the sky,
The ransom'd on the shore shall lift their song on high.

## XI. 1.

### *Men.*

Glory be to God on high,
  Who well knew, yet, knowing well,
  Lov'd His thankless Israel :
  He His hand upon the wild
  Open'd, and old Horeb smil'd ;
  Nature's face was sear and lone,
  Helpless to sustain His own,
Lo, on Sinai's rugged side
    Heaven's doors were open'd wide,
They fed on Angel's food,—but like their fathers died.

### 2.

### *Angels.*

Peace be upon earth below.
  Where the lone Bethsaida
  Looks upon the watery spray,
  Lifting up His sacred eyes,
  He brought blessings from the skies ;
  Ever to the hands anew
  Lo, th' unearthly fragments grew ;
But they who eat on that dread day,
    Death's sure and silent prey,
Liv'd but their mortal span, then pass'd from earth away.

### 3.

### *Men and Angels.*

Good will to man from God above.
  But now behold the Sacrifice,
    On which alone the soul can live ;
  Higher than Heaven th' uncounted price,
    The boon which nature cannot give ;
  Fast as His holy hand supplies,
    The blessing multiplies,
'Mid earthly vanities the Bread of Truth,
And 'mid decay and death food of immortal youth.

## XII. 1.

*Men.*

Glory be to God on high.
　From Thy skirts in mortal life
　Flow'd a stream with healing rife;
　What new blessings shall attend
　The everlasting Friend,
　Coming from His holy seat
　In the living Paraclete?
The savour of celestial things
　　In the deep bosom springs,
And Faith o'er the cold heart extends her brooding wings.

### 2.

*Angels.*

Peace be upon earth below.
　Soft as falls the heavenly dew,
　Weary nature to renew,
　Or the flakes, unearthly pure,
　Of the snowy coverture,
　Thus, too high for mortal sense,
　Christ His presence doth dispense,
Seen in diviner sympathies,
　　In sacred things made wise,
And the deep Spirit's voice of penitential sighs.

### 3.

*Men and Angels.*

Good will to man from God above.
　Jesus hath left His flock below,
　　And gone into the mount to pray
　For His disciples, left to go
　　Without Him on the stormy way:
　They, when the storm their souls shall try,
　　Shall see Him walking nigh,
And find anon upon the heavenly shore,
Where they shall go from Him on stormy waves no more.[1]

[1] This application, and the allusion in stanza II. 3, are from Origen.

Blessed is the womb that bare Thee, and the paps which Thou
hast sucked.

# ₵be Ladɣ=Chapel.

## THE SONG OF THE BLESSED VIRGIN.

*Magnificat.*

Yea, rather, blessed are they that hear the Word of God, and
keep it.

St Luke xi. 27, 28.

G

## The Lady=Chapel.

*The Song of the Blessed Virgin.*

METHOUGHT I saw 'tween walls of deep decay,
  Where thro' a mould'ring portal look'd the moon,
A solitary Vestal kneel and pray,
  Within that aged temple all alone,
  With adoration still and pensive grown ;
Thus in a tottering world, to ruin borne,
The Church doth trim her lamp, and wait the morn.

Tho' worn with watching, and with sadness clad,
  Yet, oft as break the joyous stars on high,
She with that Virgin-Mother's song is glad,
  " Tho' poor am I, Thee will I magnify ;
  Tho' no sublunar joy, nor hope have I,
Nor pillow of repose, nor worldly choice,
Yet I in God my Saviour will rejoice."

She has no voice ; but in that Virgin's song
  Divinely meditates her holier praise,
Till her aisl'd courts bear the deep notes along
  To latest time ; each evening stirs the blaze,[1]
  Filling her temple with the kindling rays,
And wakes the odorous store, till, far and nigh,
The house is fragrant with her piety.

Holiest of women ! whom the Heavenly King
  Chose for Himself, in earthly shrine inurn'd ;
Happiest of women ! for in thee the spring
  Of all our woes back to its fount was turn'd ;
Most honour'd,—cloud wherein light's centre burn'd :—
But then dishonour'd most, when thou art seen
An idol, God and man to stand between.

---

[1] The Magnificat in the Evening Service.

Alas! man's heart, in sinful consciousness,
　Some fond and frail illusion still will frame,
Which to the house of health may find access,
　Without repentance, or a sinner's shame:
　There is one only all-prevailing Name,
But unto Him none but the pure can look,
None but the penitent His presence brook.


Blessed was she on whose retirement broke
　That angel form, the star-portending morn;
And blessed she, upon whose bosom woke,
　And slept, the Eternal child, the Virgin-born,
　Who like a robe the Heaven of Heavens had worn;
But oh, more blessed, Lord, by Thy dear Name,
Is he who hears Thy word, and keeps the same.


For not in thee, thou maiden-mother mild,
　As superstition deem'd, 'tis not in thee
That we rejoice, meek mother undefil'd,
　But in our God alone both thou and we:
　For thou wast compass'd with humanity,
And Christ alone thy light, thy strength, thy tower,
Thine innocence, thy victory, thy dower.


Nor at thy feet adore we, tho' so bright
　Upon thy head the gleams of ages pour;
But with that Church rejoice, whose orient light
　Shadow'd thee forth in women fam'd of yore,
　With Hannah sung, and Miriam on the shore,
"The Lord Himself hath triumph'd gloriously,
And thrown the horse and rider in the sea."


For how can we in our own selves rejoice?
　Our better hope it hath no certain stay,
Our will no steadfastness, and when our choice
　Seems firmest set, pride shakes the tower of clay,
　Too high for lowly-building charity;
Thou on Thy Church hast shower'd down Thy love,
And we are rich in her, and Thee above.

So in her gladness we to Heaven draw near,
    Renewing her primeval sympathies,
And for ourselves keep humble-thoughted fear;
    It is the bridal of the earth and skies;
    The Queen goes forth in gold embroideries,
The light around her presence flows, and we
Discern thereby our own deep poverty.


Beneath her feet a silver anchor lies,
    She walks the clouds, and treads on human things,
With look conversing with the eternal skies,
    And step—in act to spread her rising wings,
    We seize her mantle, ere she heavenward springs,
And wait her voice,—from her no accent breaks,
Her voice is with her God, her silence speaks.


"On me Thy chosen treasures Thou hast pour'd,
    Thy never-failing riches, long foretold
To Abraham's seed,—the riches of Thy word;
    Countless as stars, many and manifold,
    Glorious are they, and of Heaven's purest gold;
Upon my head Thou settest Judah's crown,
Whose shadow lit the world, dimly foreknown.


"The princes of the world with all their state
    Have ris'n to welcome me,—to Thee I flee.
The princes of the world with all their hate
    Have ris'n to trample me,—I joy in Thee.
    Nought need I fear but lest I should be free,
When wed to Thee,—of Thine Anointing nam'd,—
And love the adult'rous world of Thee asham'd.


"My children builded for me goodly piles,
    And fill'd within with incense of sweet sound,
Spreading and rising to the starry Isles;
    But now my riches they have all unbound,
    And fain would tread my glories on the ground:
But I on Thee in my bereavement stay;—
Thou risest up, and they shall pass away.

" They clothe themselves with my magnificence,
  But it will burn their flesh like sackcloth sore ;
They, 'mid my heritage, which they dispense,
  Shall ever hunger still, and ask for more.
  I, in the nakedness of earthly store,
Thine everlasting goodness will put on,
And clothe me with Thy robe, as with the sun.


" While life is leading onward to the grave,
  Some new desire will at each turn engage ;
All pass, and leave us empty at death's cave ;—
  Pleasure, ambition, ease ;—youth, manhood, age ;
  Varying with life's advancing pilgrimage :
In Thine unchanging care I would repose,
Thine eye of watching, which doth never close.


" Nature shakes in the sun her ruffled plume,
  Rising more beauteous from her wintry state,
And renovates afresh her faded bloom :
  While her new forms are teeming at life's gate,
  Mine no fresh spring doth at death's door await ;
My mourning weeds with bitter hopes are clad,
And I in God my Saviour will be glad.


" O take me 'neath the shelter of Thy wing,
  And hide me,—of myself I am afraid,—
From myself hide me, from th' insidious spring
  Of bold high thoughts, in ambush darkly laid
  In the bad heart, as in a Stygian shade,
And leagu'd the spirit's peace to make their prey
Till I the chains of life shall fling away."

## The Parting Voluntary.

THE music dies—anon its slumbering wave
  Breaks forth, and from the opening flood-gate floats
With its full tide along the echoing nave,
  Summoning to new strength its dying notes,
Then sinks again,—like the last flash of light
Fitfully breaking ere the fall of night.

E'en thus on these our waning centuries,
  Feeble and faint compared with earlier years,
The Gospel broke, when there was seen to rise
  "The second Temple and deserving tears;" [1]
Now bursts forth the last ebbing tide,—once more
Aid our poor efforts till we gain the shore!

[1] See HERBERT.   *The Church Militant.*

# PART IV.

## The Pillars and the Windows.

## Ởḥe Ḥillars of ḥḥe Ḥaḥe.

### *Patriarchs and Prophets.*

" And he reared up the pillars . . . one on the right hand, and the other on the left."—2 CHRON. iii. 17.

" Unto them that take hold of my covenant ; even unto them will I give in Mine house and within My walls a place and a name . . . I will give them an everlasting name."—ISAIAH lvi. 4, 5.

## NOAH.

FATHER of nations ! what high thoughts endued
And arm'd thy soul with matchless fortitude,
Walking with God, in tranquil wisdom strong,
'Mid turbulence, and violence, and wrong?
Sole star descried in that tempestuous night,
Sole thing of life in that o'erwhelming blight !
It was the stronger Man, Eve's promis'd Son,
Bound Death's strong arm within thee, and put on
His armour : it was Christ in thee enshrin'd,
Stretching imploring hands to lost mankind.
In thee His feet found " rest " amid the gloom,
Noah, great name of comfort ![1]  Lights illume
The darkness, where He comes with thee to stay ;
And, on th' horizon's verge, a heavenly ray
Surrounds thee, while the black baptismal flood
Seems but to lift thee, in thy solitude,
Nearer th' aerial hall, to walk among
The stars of Heaven ;—such hopes to faith belong.
In that frail bark Christ, our Emmanuel,
Is passing o'er that more than ocean's swell,
Where seas and skies the gathering darkness fills,
Bearing His own to the celestial hills.

[1] Noah, *i.e.*, " *rest or comfort.*" See margin, Gen. v. 29.

## ABRAHAM.

GREAT emblem of the righteous, who shall stand
Girt with bright clouds on the eternal strand,
And see the world in ruin going by,
Stood Abraham, and for Sodom look'd from high.
    Behind a misty bank, skirted with gold,
The morning was contending, to unfold
And open all the gloom, where lightnings now
Retiring show'd black waters far below ;
And nothing but destruction seem'd alive,
Save where was seen a hurrying fugitive
With his two daughters, suddenly reveal'd,
And Zoar—by dark clouds again conceal'd.
    'Twas on that mount where, at last evening's close,
He stood with God ; strengthened with thought that rose
On his true soul, when importuning love
Long interceded, nor all vainly strove.
    Was it in that dread hour that Bethlehem's star
Gleam'd on thy sorrowing heart, and shew'd afar
That Coming,[1] which shall light this vale of woe ?
Sure that deep calm was thine, which spirits know
When, first awak'ning from the world's alarms,
They feel beneath the everlasting arms.

[1] John viii. 56.

## JOSEPH.

INTO some wave, which heedless night-winds rock,
The moon comes down with all her starry flock,
Her glorious imagery around her brings,
And forms a temple of celestial things.
    Thus, sweet-soul'd Joseph, as thy life ran on,
Each scene disclos'd anew th' eternal Son,
Till all thou didst, on thy meek purpose bent,
Became in thee divinely eloquent,
Presenting thee, in all that hurried by,
The mirror of some holier history.
    Tried by th' adult'rous world, temptation-proof,
But "number'd with transgressors."[1]   Now aloof
Thou sitt'st on high,—around the heathen press,
And from thine hand are fill'd with plenteousness.
But who are these? lift up thine eyes,—behold
Thy brethren, they who set at nought, and sold!
Bid all depart.—Ye little company,
Come ye around, behold me, "it is I,"[2]
Feel me, fear not! the prisoner's chain unbind:
But who is he that lingers yet behind,
"Out of due time?"[3] let ye the stranger in,
'Tis mine own Paul, mine own lov'd Benjamin.[4]

[1] St Mark xv. 28.
[3] 1 Cor. xv. 8.
[2] St Luke xxiv. 39.
[4] Phil. iii. 5.

## MOSES.

MORTAL, endow'd with more than Angel's grace !
Admitted to approach, and face to face
Converse with God ; upon the mount profound,
While the thick Darkness sentry kept around ;
Or 'neath His feet, when in the sapphire stone,
The body of the Heavens in clearness shone.[1]
All nature at thy bidding stood aghast ;
And tempests came and went with ready blast ;
And the wild sea drew up his watery bands,
To save or to destroy at thy commands.
Thus didst thou shadow forth the Living Word
Who spoke in thee, and Nature knew its Lord.
Cleft at thy rod was the obedient stone,
And waters learn'd a sweetness not their own :
But more obdurate than the hardy rock,
Less yielding than the waves, thy stubborn flock.
Thus from an ardent soul the meekest man
Came forth ; for so, in the eternal plan,
Do outward circumstance and inward toil
In stern probation join ; 'mid the turmoil
Faith sits at the soul's helm, the storm to brave,
And gains the haven against wind and wave.

[1] Exod. xxiv. 10.

## JOSHUA.

By Jericho's doom'd towers who stands on high,
With helmet, spear, and glittering panoply?
   "The Christian soldier, like a gleaming star,
   "Train'd in the wilderness to iron war."
Take off thy shoes, thy promis'd land is found,
The place thou standest on is holy ground.[1]
   "Take Thou the shield and buckler, stop the way
   "Against mine enemies ! be Thou my stay !"
I am thy rock, thy castle ; I am He
Whose feet have dried up the Egyptian sea :
Fear not, for I am with thee ; put on might ;
'Gainst thrones and powers of darkness is the fight.
   "I go, if Thou go with me ; ope the skies,
   "And lend me Heaven-attemper'd armories."
Gird Truth about thee for thy mailed dress,[2]
And for thy breastplate put on Righteousness ;
For sandals, beauteous Peace ; and for thy sword
The two-edg'd might of God's unfailing word ;
Make golden Hope thy helmet : on, and strive :—
He that o'ercometh in those courts shall live,
Whose crystal floor by heavenly shapes is trod,
   "A pillar in the temple of my God."[3]

[1] Joshua v. 15.     [2] Ephes. vi. 14-15.     [3] Rev. iii. 12.

## DAVID.

THE shepherd's staff, the sceptre, and the sword,
And Faith's victorious sling, and tuneful chord
Rife with prophetic minstrelsies, was thine,
Sweet son of Jesse ! and such grace divine
Shed beauty o'er thy ways, that thou wast prov'd
Princely and chief in all, till on thee mov'd
The eyes and hearts of men.   From heaven came down
Such rays of grace, and, forming a bright crown
Around Thy brow, mark'd Jesse's honour'd stem,
The morning star of royal Bethlehem.
   But not the shepherd's crook, sceptre, nor sword,
Nor the lov'd tones of poet's tuneful chord,
Wherein were hid prophetic mysteries,
Nor love of all men's hearts and wond'ring eyes,
Nor Sion's rising towers, nor Carmel's hill,
Nor visions which the minstrel's bosom fill,
The varying robe of day, and beauteous night,
Could meet the yearnings of his longing spright,
When his full heart upon the soothing wires
Broke forth, and pour'd therein his deep desires,—·
"Thee, Lord, alone I seek, to keep Thy door,
" And dwell within Thy courts for evermore."

## ELIJAH.

STERN, awful was thy mercy, Tishbite seer,
To close Heaven's crystal doors, for three long year,
With bands of thy strong prayer, and from men's eyes
To sweep each cloud from the offended skies.
Sure our apostate land is worse than thine,
Nor know we what to seek, what to decline.

Where wast thou wafted o'er earth's azure roof,
Borne on the whirlwind wheel and fiery hoof?
From whence thou camest forth to realms of sight,
With Moses on the mount in radiant light ;
And by the gifted eye of Faith was seen
In the stern Baptist's vest and awful mien.

From Heaven's calm mansions and ethereal cell,
Where thou beyond the summer clouds dost dwell,
Wilt thou again upon the earth appear,
In living form, or type, or vision clear,
To harbinger the great Elisha's sway,
The coming in of the eternal day?

Full much we need thee, and thy mantle strong,
To part the rising waters ! Envious wrong
And filial disobedience [1] lift on high
Their swelling waves, and seem to threat the sky.

[1] Malachi iv. 6.

## ELISHA.

THE Great Elisha may I call Thy name,
Eternal Saviour, and be free from blame?
E'en as the sun, in things of meanest worth,
His coming and his going shadows forth
From image unto image, so art Thou
Full oft anew reveal'd ; Elijah now
Lone wandering, then Elisha's loftier seat,
The Son of man, and then the Paraclete.[1]
   Thou wast mysterious veil'd in growing bread ;[2]
Thou in the sacramental oil didst shed
Thine undiminish'd Spirit, flowing o'er
The widow'd Church's vessels evermore.[3]
   It is Thy figure in the dead man's bones,
Where charnel'd death life-giving[4] virtue owns ;
'Tis Thou in unapproached purity,
Who smit'st Thy foes with eyes that cannot see :[5]
While Thine own friends discern a rampart round,
Where cars and horse of living flame abound.
It was Thy word turn'd the baptismal wave
Of Jordan to Thy blood, with power to save.[6]
May we in that sure word that cannot fail,
Strike seven times, and seven times prevail ![7]

---

[1] Elijah seems a type of Christ in the days of His flesh ; Elisha in His Church.
[2] 2 Kings iv. 44.          [3] Ibid. iv. 6.          [4] Ibid. xiii. 21.
[5] Ibid. vi. 18 ; and John xii. 40.          [6] Ibid. v. 10, 14.
[7] 2 Kings xiii. 19.

## ISAIAH.

DEEP-VISION'D son of Amoz ! with fix'd gaze
And full-tranc'd eyelid, when the illumin'd rays
Fell on thy heart and to thy ravish'd sense
Rose future scenes hid in Omnipotence :—
    Whether when hell was moved, and from its throne
Arose to greet the crown-less Babylon,[1]
Or lifted earth, and the descending sky
In vocal gladness blend, as feeling nigh
The coming of th' eternal Jubilee ;
And mountains find a voice, and the glad sea
Listens with all his isles ;[2] or from thy brow
A hand unseen the curtain lifts, and, lo,
Dread judgments lower o'er guilty Israel ;
And, by near shadows made more visible,
Bright scenes come forth ; like landscapes, baffling thought,
Pictur'd afar on hanging clouds, and brought
To a strange nearness ; fairer than the state
Which evening pours upon Heaven's western gate,
Or music opens, with a touch of light
Bringing lost Eden on the inward sight.[3]
    At every turn the Man of Sorrow[4] stands,
Bearing the key[5] to those unearthly lands.

[1] Isaiah xiv. 9.    [2] Ibid. xiii. 10-12.    [3] Ibid. li. 3.
[4] Ibid. liii. 3.    [5] Ibid. lv. 3 ; comp. Rev. iii. 7.

## JEREMIAH.

" Come, see, was ever sorrow like to mine ? " [1]
What more than human woe, dread Voice, is thine,
While armed shapes of terror throng the crowd,
Which over Judah brings destruction's shroud ? [2]
Carrying our griefs, and supplicating still,
It is the Man of sorrows [3] climbs the hill
Of Calvary : o'er Salem shedding tears, [4]
In Anathoth's sad Seer He witness bears.
    " Come, see, was ever sorrow like to mine ? "
From age to age still sounds that voice divine,
Still Sion's virgin daughter heaves the sigh,
    " Say, is it nought to you, ye that pass by ? "
Ye Heavens, be hung with sackcloth, and thou earth
Shorn of thy beauty ! let the robe of dearth
Clothe the green mountains ! they their Maker own,
But of mine Israel I am not known.
"Seek ye the ancient paths, and ye shall live ; " [5]
But they cry out, "We will not."   I would strive,
But strong-arm'd vengeance, as it grows more deep,
Holds them in her embrace and lays asleep,
While I o'er your destruction watch and pine,—
" Come, see, was ever sorrow like to mine ? "

[1] Lam. i. 12.        [2] Jer. iv. 13.        [3] Lam. iii. 1.
[4] Jer. ix. 1 ; comp. Luke xix. 41.        [5] Ibid. vi. 16.

## EZEKIEL.

LEND me the key which opes the secret cells,
Where, in His words and works, the Godhead dwells.
 As nearer we approach Him, all things throng
Vocal with heavenly language, and a tongue
Speaking in figure, where the East descries
The glowing footsteps of th' unfolded skies.
 By Chebar's flood, around the Prophet come
Dread speaking faces, peopling all the gloom,
And Cherubim with Cherubim do ply
Their wheeling wings, and fiery shapes pass by.
Or, with the swiftness of a flying star,
He in Jerusalem is found afar.[1]
Now Egypt, the great dragon, netted lies
'Mid his own waters ;[2] or the seas arise
O'er Tyre, the princely ship that walk'd the waves ;[3]
Now Lebanon's Cedar the strong tempest braves.[4]
 E'en now, as then, in images of fire
Men see the flashes of th' Almighty's ire,
Admire, and tremble not ; they come around
And listen to the Church, as to the sound
Of a sweet lovely song, or tuneful reed,
And hear her awful voice, but do not heed.[5]

---

[1] Ezek. xl. 2.     [2] Ibid. xxxii. 3.     [3] Ibid. xxvii. 26
[4] Ibid. xvii. 23     [5] Ibid. xxxii. 32.

## DANIEL.

WE sit beside the streams of Babylon,
'Neath willowy shades, and hang our harps thereon,
Rememb'ring Sion.   What strong cords of love
Shall bind the exile to his home above?
    Lov'd intercessor, thou the arts canst tell
Which draw from Heaven that all-constraining spell;
Whether thou sitt'st by Hiddekel's broad stream,
Or where on Ulai sleeps the noonday beam;
Or stand'st with outstretch'd hands in palace hall,
Where fiery characters night's shades appal.
    It is in steadfast prayer, the earnest eyes
Set toward the living temple of the skies, —
Stern hardihood, 'mid fasts and watches won,—
And that pure lamp that shall outshine the sun,
The virgin soul,—these, in thy breast inurn'd,
All glowing thoughts to love seraphic turn'd :
Until an ear in wakeful trance was given,
Converse to hold with pursuivants of Heaven;
An eye, the shapes in Time's dark womb to scan
And see amid the clouds the Son of Man;
A better boon than sons or daughters fair,
To find a place within God's House of Prayer.[1]

[1] Isaiah lvi. 4, 5.

## The Pillars of the Choir.

### *Apostles.*

"Him that overcometh will I make a pillar in the temple of my God."—REV. iii. 12.

"And the wall of the City had twelve foundations; and in them the names of the twelve Apostles of the Lamb."—REV. xxi. 14.

## ST PETER.

WITH what full eyes of wonder wast thou bent
Upon each passing look, each act intent,[1]
Fix'd on the Son of Man with earnest gaze,
While on thy heart the Father shed His rays,
Till gradual He disclos'd the mighty whole,
And the dread Godhead open'd on thy soul!
  As step by step thou followedst close around
And nearest, deeper spells thy spirit bound,
Watching each light, and shade, and speaking glance,
That mark'd thy Master's awful countenance:
Till, unreveal'd of man, thy God and Lord
Thy tongue acknowledg'd, and thy heart ador'd;
And thou wast meet to climb unto the fount
Of glory, seen on Tabor's secret mount.
Thence to that faith, as to a firm-set rock,
With thee the ransom'd of all ages flock,
Where the dread Twelve are met, who hold the keys
Which ope and close Heaven's ivory palaces.
  Thus some fair star, on its ethereal way,
Seems gazing on the golden orb of day,
And drinks his radiance, till itself, made bright,
When the Sun sinks, for others lights the night.

---

[1] See Tracts for the Times, No. 80. p. 31.

## ST ANDREW.

Oʜ that, ere death shall close my eyes in sleep,
I might behold that Galilean deep,
Sun-gilded waves, and hill-embosom'd strand,
Where Andrew dwelt with his fraternal band !
Andrew, who saw and heard the Living Word,
And came, and then brought Peter to the Lord :
Andrew, next added to that favour'd three,[1]
School'd in Christ's lore upon their native sea.
  Blest sight! to see those heights which round them clos'd,
When holy eyes on their dark shapes repos'd ;
To watch those gales which came upon the deep,
When in that hold their Lord was laid asleep ;
To see those rocks where dwelt their thoughts of home,
And 'neath that glowing firmament to roam,
Move on the sea they moved on, and behold
The moon and stars which they beheld of old !
  But ah, far more, when death hath clos'd my eyes,
Might I but see, beyond those eastern skies,
By Andrew led, where, round our Saviour's feet,
The Holy Twelve in sweet communion meet
In their last haven, on that stable shore,
Beside that crystal sea for evermore !

[1] See St Mark xiii. 3.

## ST JAMES THE GREAT.

ONE of that chosen three, who found such grace
To be admitted to the secret place
Of His life-giving Presence, from the sight
Of the rude world there lost in radiant light.
Nor know we aught of thee,—the great and good,
The sun of thunder, and baptiz'd in blood,—
Nor thought, nor word, nor deed.   'Tis ever so :
In shadow of his Hand He hides below
Those who His Presence seek ; Himself unseen
And His good Angels, in that blissful skreen
He gathers them in silence, to abide
Beneath His shrouding wings and sheltering side.
Tho' visibly beheld 'mid suffering men,
His name is "Secret ; " [1] nor can mortals ken
His Sion's haunts, the mount invisible
Where He 'mid Saints and Angels deigns to dwell.
   Whether allow'd to Tabor's secret height,
Or sorrows of Gethsemane, or sight
And solemn chambers of relenting death,
Where Heaven's full power is seen o'er parting breath ; [2]
The world but sees them share His humbling rod
Unto the door ;—then leaves them with their God.

[1] Judges xiii. 18. '
[2] The Transfiguration, the Agony in the garden, and the raising of Jairus's daughter, were the occasions when St Peter, St James, and St John, were alone present.

## ST JOHN.

"AMEN.   E'en so, Lord Jesus, come."   O why
Tarry so long Thy chariot-wheels, while I,
I only yet remain, and, one by one,
The tried companions of Thy Love are gone!
And I, all dearest treasures gone before,
Am left upon the solitary shore?
   So better may I learn "Thy will be done;"
For whom have I in Heaven, but Thee alone?
And whom have I on earth, but only Thee?
Therefore, with one foot on the stormy sea,
And one foot fix'd on the eternal strand,
Thou hold'st me by Thy never-failing hand.
Before Thy face, that bringeth in the day,
The mountains and the hills shall flee away,
The sun and stars in darkness make their bed,
And forth the Bridal City shall be led;
For Thy blest City needs not sun or moon,
But in Thy face hath its unwaning noon.[1]
Therefore alone in Thy eternal Love
I seek for refuge; Thee in Heaven above,
And Thee below! Blest they who, day and night
Serve Thee, and have their dwelling in Thy sight!

[1] Rev. xxi. 23.

## ST PHILIP.

HAST Thou so long been with us, gracious Lord,
And yet have we not known Thee?[1] while Thy word
Within us and about us wraps around,
Impalpable as th' air? Thine eye is found
In th' heart of hearts, and Thy sustaining hand ;
And all events, arrang'd at Thy command,
Are but th' unfoldings of a Father's care,
Unsought for, and responsive to our prayer,—
And yet have we not known Thee? have we brought
Others to Thee,[2] and Thy true wisdom taught,—
And yet not known thee?   By our home retreat,
Our own Bethsaida,[3] " Have ye here no meat?"
Thou seem'st to say, that so Thou mightest lead
To feel our own deep want, in that our need,
Of all true bread that satisfies, that we
Might turn, and hang our famish'd souls on Thee ;
Thousands at Thy good word with food abound,
And shew that Thy live presence dwells around,—
And yet have we not known Thee? have not known
The all-transcending circle and the crown
Of Thy deep Love?—still know Thee not, nor find
The Father's image within Thee enshrin'd?[4]

---

[1] St John xiv. 9.     [2] Ibid. xii. 22.
[3] Ibid. vi. 5.     [4] Ibid. xiv. 10.

## ST BARTHOLOMEW.

COME forth, Nathanael, from the fig-tree's shade,
And see, where, down yon mountain's solemn glade,
The lowly Nazareth, in the summer even,
Shines in the sunbeams, like a gate of Heaven!
'Mid those poor walls, Heaven opens to thy prayer,
And Angels pass upon the crystal stair.
    And who within that Tabernacle's light
Shall dwell, but thou, the guileless Israelite?[1]
Thine is the art of artless souls, true seer!
To know thy God in all things standing near.
Divine prerogative! The blameless soul,
Its own simplicity, its sweet control,
Leads on, and, like a guardian spirit, brings
Into the palace of the King of kings,[2]
The Mount of God. To Him all nature stirs,
Ranging herself in glowing characters;
Seen thro' Faith's light'ning mirror, blooming skies
Come down on earth and sea, like vernal dyes,
Speaking of Resurrection;—all are rife
And animate with forms of beauteous life,
Unseen before; 'mid busiest scenes below,
The messengers of Mercy come and go.

---

[1] Ps. xv. 1 : comp. St John i. 47.　　　[2] St Matt. v. 8.

## ST MATTHEW.

Nor Pharisaic school, nor harness'd train
Of Roman state, nor pow'r, nor thoughtful gain,
Nor breezy lake, where circling mountains rise,
Nor Lebanon's snowy top in summer skies,
Could to thy longing eyes afford repose,
Good Levi, till they found the Man of woes!
  Beneath thy lowly roof I see Him come,[1]
An honour'd guest; the Pharisee's stern gloom
Sitting aloof,—in calm and humble gaze
The Galilean twelve,—th' half-pleas'd amaze
Of Publicans,—and mourning Eremite
Shrinking apart: yet seen, or out of sight,
Manifold words of wisdom find them out,
And in each heart an eye that looks throughout.
  But, lo, again his hospitable store
Levi prepares, unfolding wide the door
Of His blest Gospel, 'neath whose sacred roof
All may behold the Christ, and learn by proof.
E'en now, as then, within each secret soul
An eye is found; seek we or shun control,
All see the Son of Man; each doth invest
His form with hues deep drawn from His own breast.

[1] St Luke v. 29, &c.

## ST THOMAS.

BLESSED are they who, needing no loud sign [1]
Of reason, or felt proof, or voice divine,
Believing love ; and, loving, ask not sight !
They on the bosom of the Infinite
Have been, and there in Faith for ever lie ;
Believe because they love, and ask not why :
But on His bosom lie they all day long,
And drink His words, and are refresh'd and strong ;
Thro' all Thy works, Thee, Lord, at every turn,
Thro' all Thy Word, Thee and Thy Cross discern ;
Shrine within shrine, and hall encircling hall,
Pass unto Thee, to Thee, the All in All.
    Thine too are they, of ruder sense, who deem
Such thoughts but fancies of the mystic's dream ;
Then, to their questioning and ruder sense,
In palpable and solemn evidence
Thy presence breaks, in providential change
Defying thought, or visitation strange :
They see and feel Thy hands and pierced side,
Worship, and their adoring heads would hide.
Such dwell in Thy blest courts, and see Thy face,
But not most near Thine altar have their place.

[1] St John xx. 29. ˅

## ST JAMES THE LESS.

WHERE death's deep shade the ruin'd Salem shrouds,
A covenanted bow amid the clouds
Opens a brighter city to disclose,
Wherein the Son of Man, in dread repose,
Is walking 'mid the candlesticks of gold,
And the seven stars in His right hand doth hold.[1]
First in the kingdom of the Crucified,
Unto the Son of God in flesh allied,
And more allied in suffering, James, the Just,
Bears the new keys of Apostolic trust.[2]
And well we deem that 'twas thine only pride
To bear the Cross on which thy Master died,
In daily dying; by self-chast'ning care,
Vigil, and fast, to unloose the wings of Prayer
From bodily weight, and win Faith's hallow'd spell,
Which breaks from captive souls the chains of hell.[3]
So putt'st thou on Christ's loyal poverty,
Looking thro' earth, as with an Angel's eye,
With all its wealth like the fair flow'ring grass,
Whereon Christ's words of woe already pass
Like some hot burning wind : while Patience mild
Drinks Heaven's pure light, and vigour undefil'd.[4]

---

[1] Rev. ii. 1.  [2] The first Bishop of Jerusalem.
[3] St Mark ix. 29.  [4] St James i. 10-12.

## ST JUDE.

ONE glory kindles night's aërial blue,
But clothes each star with its distinctive hue ;
One light from crystal dew-drops on the thorn
Calls forth the varied jewels of the morn :
And, in that little band of Jesus blest,
To whom our Lord " Himself did manifest,"
And who on Him in answ'ring love are bent,
Faith doth in each a varying form present.
 Thus that deep voice, O Jude, is all thine own,
Tho' Christ is heard in thy dread warning tone,
And speaks in thee, exhorting with arm'd [1] heed
To wrestle for the everlasting Creed.
 Unfolding ever to our feeble sight
In endless form, we see the Infinite ;
Nor doth the varied human countenance,
So manifold in shape and speaking glance,
Range through more boundless changes, than doth Love
In spirits which are born of God above.
 Thus, Lord, when, from Thy vessels of rude clay,
Thou makest up Thy jewels on that day,
Their diverse hues, with Thy pure lustre sown,
Shall blend to form Thy many-colour'd crown.

---

[1] 'Επαγωνίζεσθαι.  St Jude, ver. 3.

## ST SIMON.

O Thou, Who art th' eternal Corner-stone,
And bearest up Heaven's pillar'd frame alone ;
Thou art the Light that fills each living gem,
Which glimmers in Thy Church's diadem !
Thou art her Crown : the stars which round her shine
Are but the effulgence of Thy fire divine ;
Thy Wisdom in the Twelve made manifest,
The Urim and the Thummim on Thy breast,
Sole Living Priest ! 'twas Thy heart-glowing light
That burn'd within the zealous Canaanite ;
Thou who didst drive the buyers to the door,
And with Thy mantle sweep Thy Father's floor !
O wrath most merciful ! portentous sign
Of Thy Last Coming, arm'd with wrath divine !
  Do Thou my heart with holy zeal control,
And purify the temple of my soul,
Drive each foul thought with Thine uplifted rod,
Which stains the floor Thy holy feet have trod ;
A den of evil fancies, whence arise
Far other fumes than love of Thee supplies :—
Oh, cleanse my heart betimes, ere Thou shalt come
And sweep Thy temple with eternal doom !

## ST MATTHIAS.

FROM Abraham's breast, 'mid heavenly towers on high,
Death's lake is seen, and heard the dismal cry;
From Salem's heights, dread Sodom's sea of doom
Is o'er the hills descried in fiery gloom :
'Mid that small band, for Heaven's high mandate seal'd,
Hell opens, and a Judas is reveal'd.
   Dread thought of terror ! Heaven the rescued crown
Holds, and on just Matthias lets it down ;
Sent forth of Him Who was sent forth of God,
And arm'd with nought but His supporting rod.[1]
   Oh, by that Cross on which Thou deign'st to die,
Let that staff bear me Death's dark valley by !—[2]
Thine was the Patriarch's staff, when Jordan's strand
He pass'd, and thence return'd a two-fold band ;—[3]
Thine was the staff Elisha sent before,
The staff of health which false Gehazi bore.[4]
   From this new morn until th' eternal Day,
That pastoral staff must be the pilgrim's stay ;
From this new morn, when, from its wintry blight,
Springs the new year, and day is mast'ring night.[5]
Still, wheresoe'er the grounded staff shall pass,[6]
The sea divides,—wide opes the watery mass.

[1] St Mark vi. 8, "nothing . . save a *staff* only."
[2] Ps. xxiii. 4.        [3] Gen. xxxii. 10.        [4] 2 Kings iv. 31.
[5] St Matthias was ordained at the first Easter.
[6] Isaiah xxx. 32.

## The Western Window.

### *The Nativity.*

"And the City had no need of the Sun, neither of the Moon, to shine in it : for the glory of God did lighten it, and the Lamb is the light thereof." REV. xxi. 23.

SWEET sounds on high this night have birth,
    And sounds as sweet on earth ;
Where Heaven is heard, from a bright stooping cloud,
    With music ringing loud :
Less than angelic voice might well be mute,
Such more than Heavenly theme to suit.

    The stars of night are drawing near,
        Each on his crystal sphere,
        That Angel's voice to hear ;
        And, from their mazy rout,
        That walks the Heavens about,
        They send a silver scout,
        A glowing pursuivant,
        To lead the hearts and eyes
        Of men celestial wise,
    To where, around the homely shed of want,
The infinite deep skies their legion'd squadrons plant. ·

    See, the rays, His brows adorning,
    Are the light of endless morning,
    From that lowly cradle shining ;
    O'er the Heaven-born Babe reclining,
    With a more than speaking gaze
    Blending joy with dread amaze,
    Hangs the holy Mother-maid :
    While, within the darker shade,
    Comes there round a wond'ring group,—
    Some gaze, and some adoring stoop ;
    And the ox with horned brow
    Stands beside ; and, bending low,

H

He whose shoulders graven deep
Aye his Master's mark shall keep,
Unconscious that their Lord is there,
Their heritage of pain to bear.

See throughout the casement drear
The old mountains standing near :
Is it Heaven, or is it earth,
Which is gathering round His birth ?
For within the womb of night
There hath sprung unwonted light :
Lo, where, startled at the day,
Darkness looks into the room :
And, afar, within the gloom
War and Rapine haste away
From light, around His childhood streaming ;
And, with half-averted brow,
Pride is hast'ning down below,
'Mid the darker shadows gleaming.

Hasten with light-footed glee,
Let us join the jubilee,
Where the shepherd and the king,
And angelic squadrons sing ;—
Over sea, and over land,
Knitted in one brother's band ;
Where the joyous accents run,
Never ending, ne'er begun,
And the Heavens take up the song,
With harmonious thunders strong,
And twice ten thousand worlds the wondrous theme prolong.

# The Side Windows.

## ANCIENT FATHERS.

" Behold, I will lay thy stones with fair colours, and lay thy founda·
tions with sapphires ; and I will make thy windows of agates."—
ISAIAH liv. 11, 12.

" And they that be wise shall shine as the brightness of the firma·
ment."—DANIEL xii. 3.

## The Side Windows.

*Ancient Fathers.*

---

### CLEMENT OF ROME.

[Bishop of Rome, author of an Epistle to the Corinthians, reproving the divisions which were afflicting the Church there. He was the first of the Roman bishops whose writings have come down to us, and he wrote, as our poet reminds us, in a time of persecution, namely, that of Domitian.]

As heavenly blue breaks on a troubled deep,
    A voice of gentle blame,
From the calm grave where Paul and Peter sleep,
    Unto their children came,
From Rome to Corinth.   O'er the rising din
    It swell'd, as from their purer seats above,
And, like a solemn undersound therein,
    Paul's moving tone.   It was thy watchful love,
Clement, whose name is in the book of life ; [1]
The while thy Church, true to Heaven's sacred mould,
    'Mid persecution, poverty, and strife,
Glorious within, and wrought of purest gold,
Began 'mid hanging mists her greatness to unfold.

---

[1] Phil. iv. 3.

## IGNATIUS.

[Bishop of Antioch, sent to Rome for martyrdom. On his way he came to several places which are named in the Revelation. The " burning hardihood " has reference to the joy which filled his soul at the expectation of martyrdom, so that he wrote to the Church at Rome, to beg them not to endeavour to save him from death.]

As, one by one, stars on the eastern space
    Come forth, while daylight fades,
And greet each other to their heavenly place,
    Thus, while death's deepening shades
Darken around thy steps in stranger lands,
    Sweet awful memories of thine own St John
Wake round thee ; martyr'd Peter beckoning stands,
    And stirs again the Spirit's benison
Giv'n thro' his hands : upon the selfsame road,
Lo, the bright footsteps of the death-bound Paul !
Thy soul is fann'd to burning hardihood ;
We hear in thee the Bridegroom's warning call,
    And full of glowing life thy dying accents fall.

## POLYCARP.

[Bishop of Smyrna, martyred A.D. 147. The poet assumes that he is " the Angel of the Church of Smyrna," addressed in Rev. ii., but this must be regarded as very doubtful.]

ANGEL of Smyrna, child of John,
And friend of that beloved one,
Belov'd of Him Whose love is life,
How didst thou, left to worldly strife,
Bear with thee, as in holiest trance,
The music of that countenance,
Which spoke the wisdom of the skies
And his own Master's charities?
Again that voice [1] from Patmos came
With auguries of thy couch of flame,[2]
And bore his Saviour's praise to thee,
Whose praise is immortality,—
" To death be faithful Me to own,
"And I will give to thee life's never-fading crown."

[1] Rev. ii. 8. " Unto the Angel of the Church in Smyrna write," &c.
[2] He had dreamed three days before his martyrdom, that he was sleeping on a pillow of fire.

# JUSTIN.

[The first Christian "Apologist." Born at Sychem in Samaria, martyred probably about A.D. 163. His principal writings are his two Apologies, and his "Dialogue with Trypho" the Jew. From the latter work is derived the incident of the following poem.]

UPON the solitary shore
Stood Justin, wrapt in Plato's lore,
Seeking, with self-abstracted mind,
The beatific light to find.
A grey-hair'd man on that lone wild,
With venerable aspect mild,
Before him came, and bade him scan
Visions too high for sinful man :—
" Pray thou to God both day and night
"To ope to thee the gates of light,
" Reveal'd of God in Christ alone." [1]
In Justin's breast a fire was sown ;—
Borne heavenward in that glowing flame
His mantle he let fall, a Martyr's honour'd name.

[1] Dialog. cum Tryph., p. 218.

## IRENÆUS.

[Bishop of Lyons from A.D. 177 till about the end of the century. A native of Smyrna and disciple of Polycarp. He was very strenuous in his warfare against heresies and in preserving peace in his diocese.]

FROM new-born Lyons oft thy memory turn'd
Unto the earlier East, and fondly yearn'd
For Polycarp and Smyrna, and the youth
Of grave Religion fair.   But wakeful Truth
Within Tradition's [1] holy citadel
Kept watch, and her stamp'd treasures guarded well,
Her Apostolic store ; thou by her light
Didst guide the bark amid the gathering night
Of heresies, and th' helm didst sternly hold,
Lifting a martyr's voice, serene and bold.
Would that again thy city of the Rhone
Might break her Roman bonds, and thee her champion own !

[1] See passages from Irenæus quoted by Mr Keble, in his Sermon on Primitive Tradition, p. 24, first edition.

## TERTULLIAN.

[Priest of Carthage ; the first Latin writer whose works we possess. He was a most powerful writer, but in his zeal against heresy he fell into the heresy of Montanus, and to this the poem has reference.]

How art thou fallen ! seeking, 'mid the stars
To set thy nest ; unloos'd from fleshly bars,
Striving the chasten'd soul " to wind too high "
For one encompass'd with humanity !
Could not thy Mother's milk and quiet breast
Suffice thee, nurturing to Eden's rest ?
Thou wast her glory ; and the fiend of pride
Ne'er could have won thee from her peaceful side,
Were he not trick'd in guise of lowliness.
Thou art her glory still ; and she no less
Puts on the armouries of thy soberer soul,
And reads from thy sad fall her lesson of control.

## CLEMENT OF ALEXANDRIA.[1]

[The great Platonist father, who presided over the Catechetical School
of Alexandria at the end of the second century. Of some of his writings
only fragments are preserved, but his " Address to the Greeks," the
" Stromata," and " The Tutor " almost entirely remain.]

METHOUGHT I saw a face divinely fair,
 With nought of earthly passion ; the mild beam
 Of whose bright eye did in mute converse seem
With other countenances, and they were,
 Gazing on her, made beautiful. Their theme
Was One that had gone up the heavenly stair,
And left a fragrance on this lower air,
 The contemplation of His Love supreme.
And that high form held forth to me a hand :—
It was celestial Wisdom, whose calm brow
 Did of those earthly Sciences inquire,
If they had of His glory aught retain'd :—
 Yes ! I would be admitted to your choir,
That I may nothing love on earth below.

[1] These thoughts are suggested by the Stromata, b. v. 555.

## ORIGEN.[1]

[This great Alexandrian father (b. 185 ; d. 253) was famous for his labours in editing and commenting upon Holy Scripture. The fears expressed by the poet are occasioned by the supposed danger of his over fondness for allegorising Holy Scripture, and also of his hope for the final salvation of all men.]

INTO God's word as in a palace fair,
  Thou leadest on and on, while still, beyond
Each chamber, touch'd by holy Wisdom's Wand,
Another opes, more beautiful and rare ;
And thou in each art kneeling down in prayer,
  From link to link of that mysterious bond
Seeking for Christ ; but oh, I fear thy fond
And beautiful torch, that with so bright a glare
  Lighteth up all things, lest thy Heaven-lit brand
And thy serene Philosophy divine
Should take the colourings of earthly thought,
And I, by their sweet images o'erwrought,
  Led by weak Fancy, should let go Truth's hand,
And miss the way into the inner shrine.

[1] On reading his Commentaries on Scripture.

## CYPRIAN.[1]

[Bishop of Carthage, cir. 248-261, martyred in the Decian persecution. His works were published in the Oxford "Library of the Fathers," and to this reference is made in line 8. It was published about the same time as the poem.]

BUT who is this upon the pictur'd pane
    With stole deep-dyed in blood,
No countenance amid that Saintly train
    Of sterner fortitude?
Cyprian, Saint, Bishop, Martyr ! forth he stands
    In the rich glow of Afric's burning sky,
To us of other tongues and other lands
    In our own native eloquence brought nigh.[2]
To thee, another Carthage, he comes near,
    Tyre of the Western wave, in warning brought !
Thence mayst thou learn a sterner faith and fear,
    For hues of Heaven Time cannot bring to nought,
Still fresh the Martyr's blood flows in each glowing thought.

[[1] The following by Keble, appeared in the earliest Editions instead of the above :—

    The lions prowl around, thy grave to guard,
      And Moslem prayers profane
    At morn and eve come sounding ; yet, unscar'd,
      Thy Holy Shades remain ;—
    Cyprian, the chief of watchmen, wise and bold,
      Trusting the lore of his own loyal heart,
    And Cyprian's Master, as in age high-soul'd,
      Yet choosing as in youth, the better part.
    There, too, unwearied Austin, thy keen gaze
      On Atlas' steep, a thousand years and more,
    Dwells, waiting for the first rekindling rays,
      When Truth upon the solitary shore
    For the fall'n West may light his beacon as of yore.]

[2] The Oxford Translation of his works.

## DIONYSIUS OF ALEXANDRIA.

[Bishop of Alexandria, cir. 247-265. He wrote treatises on Nature and on the Promises, one or two controversial works, and commentaries on Ecclesiastes and St Luke. Only fragments of any of them remain.]

THO' thy sweet eloquent spirit knew no chains
    In thought's o'erflowing store,
Lost are thy letter'd toils,—scarce aught remains,—
    Lost on Oblivion's shore !
Yet not all lost; but laid upon His breast
    In whom they have their origin and end.
Part He conceals, and part makes manifest,
    Each as may best to His good purpose tend.
It matters not,—for we must soon be gone,
    And things of earth most cherish'd, are like hues
Of sun-set, fading from us one by one,
    Tho' heavenly rays a passing grace infuse ;
Till ours and our own selves we in His Being lose.

## HIPPOLYTUS.

[It is very remarkable that of this Saint, who in the beginning of the third century was the most learned member of the Roman Church, so little is known. That he was a bishop and martyr seems to have been universally believed by early Christian writers, but the place of his see is a question which has exercised some of the most learned Church writers. In 1842 a copy of a work written by him, which was known to have been so written, but was supposed to be lost, was discovered in the monastery of Mount Athos. It is his treatise against Heresies.]

MARTYR and Bishop, honour'd name,
　Thine earthly place unknown,
Whom East and West alike may claim,
　But neither prove their own !

Thine eye seems watching everywhere,
　And everywhere divines
The Antichrist approaching near,
　'Mid dread portending signs.

Thus like a spirit, with subtle grace,
　Thou thro' all lands dost glide !
For he who nowhere hath his place
　Doth everywhere abide ;

Of Antichrist meet harbinger :—
　For 'neath each distant sky
He nor in time nor place can err,
　Who deems Christ's coming nigh.

## GREGORY THAUMATURGUS.

[Born in 210. Bishop of Cæsarea, cir. 233-270. His repute as having miraculous gifts, "cannot," says Dr Reynolds, "be set down as exclusively due to the credulousness of the age, for, as Lardner remarked, such writers as Basil, Jerome, and Theodoret, to say nothing of Gregory of Nyssa, distinguished this particular Bishop from all others, as a man of apostolic signs and wonders."]

THINE Angel led thee by the hand
  To thy lov'd Origen,
Taught to forget thy father's land,
  And sit with holy men.

Thro' varied wilds of knowledge fair
  He lured to sacred lore,
And bade thee knock with earnest prayer,
  Till faith should ope the door.[1]

And well I ween that at Heaven-gate
  Thy hand did knock, till Love
Came forth, all arm'd with unseen state,
  The mountains to remove.

For thou art known to latest time
  The "wonder-working" sage,
Who could a rude barbaric clime
  To Christian love engage.

See Origen's letter to Gregory.

## ATHANASIUS.

[Archbishop of Alexandria (b. 296; d. 373.) The grandest contro-
versialist among the early fathers. The "troubles" referred to are his
great conflicts with the Arians, who, says Hooker, "never suffered
him till the last hour of his life in this world to enjoy the comfort of a
peaceable day." The last line refers to the fact that the Athanasian
Creed is named after him.]

A SEA of troubles tried thee, till at length,
  Borne back by thy strong sinew, they uprear'd
Thy might, and sternly bore thee in thy strength
  Onward, till on the Eternal Rock appear'd
  Truth's loyal champion, to all time rever'd.

Great Athanasius! beaten by wild breath
  Of calumny, of exile, and of wrong,
Thou wert familiar grown with frowning Death,
  Looking him in the face all thy life long,
  Till thou and he were friends, and thou wert strong.

The " Eye of Alexandria," [1] rais'd on high,
  Unto all Christendom a beacon light:
Thou from our tossing waves, and stormy sky,
  Art in thy peaceful haven hid from sight;
  But still thy name hath leave to guide us thro' the night.

[1 This expression is taken from an Epistle of Basil. " He stands,
like the Pharos, on his lofty watch-tower of speculation, seeing with
his ubiquitous glance what is passing throughout this world. He
overlooks the wide stormy ocean, where there is a vast fleet at sea."
—(Quoted in Stanley's Eastern Church, p. 302.)]

## AMBROSE.

[Bishop of Milan from 374 to 397.]

To thee an eye to trace out the third Heaven
  In holy writ, and see the mercy-throne,—
A brother's love,[1]—a poet's lyre was given,[2]
  But yet o'er all thy gifts the Pastor shone,
  To God's high altar bound, no more thine own.

I see thee stand before the injur'd shrine,[3]
  While Theodosius to thy stern decree
Falls down, and owns the keys and power divine :
  For kings that fain her nursing-sires would be,
  To the Eternal Bride must bow the knee.[4]

I see thee thron'd upon the Teacher's seat,—
  And 'mid the crowd a silent wand'rer steal :[5]
In his sad breast, while sitting at thy feet,
  ·  The Father doth th' eternal Son reveal,
And Austin from thy hands receives the Spirit's seal.

[1 This refers to his deep affection for his brother Satyrus and his sister Marcellina.]

[2 His poetic and musical gifts were evidently of a very high order. Many hymns which are attributed to him are not really his—*e.g.*, the *Te Deum*. But there is no reasonable doubt that " *Veni Redemptor Gentium*," " *Æterne rerum Conditor*," " *O lux beata Trinitas*," are his.]

[3 The splendid act of discipline by which he brought the Emperor Theodosius to repentance for the massacre of Thessalonica is one of the best known facts of history.]

4 Isaiah lix. 23.

[5 The " Silent Wanderer " was Augustine. He came while still in mental anxiety and darkness to hear Ambrose preach, was converted to the faith, and baptized by Ambrose.]

# BASIL.

[Bishop of Cæsarea in Cappadocia (born 329, died 379).   It was during his priesthood that a rupture with Eusebius, his predecessor in the see, caused him to retire with his friend Gregory Nazianzen to the solitude of Pontus, where he remained for three years in charge of the monasteries which he had himself founded.]


BEAUTIFUL flowers round Wisdom's secret well
   Deep holy thoughts of penitential lore,
   And dress'd with images from Nature's store,
Handmaid of Piety! Like thine own cell,
By Pontic mountain wilds and shaggy fell,
   Great Basil! there, within thy lonely door,
Watching, and Fast, and Prayer, and Penance dwell,
And sternly-nurs'd Affections heavenward soar.
Without are setting suns and summer skies,
Ravine, rock, wood, and fountain melodies;
   And Earth and Heaven, holding communion sweet,
   Teem with wild beauty.   Such thy calm retreat,
   Blest Saint! and of thyself an emblem meet,
All fair without, within all stern and wise.

# GREGORY NAZIANZEN.

[A native of Nazianzus, in Cappadocia. His mother, Nonna, believing him to be given to her in answer to prayer, dedicated him to the Lord in infancy. He became Archbishop of Constantinople in 380, and died in 390.]

MEEK Nazianzen, whom a mother's love
  Vow'd from the womb, a Christian Nazarite !
  A friend's, a brother's care fill'd thy calm sprite,
And filial grace serene : the hallowing Dove
Then open'd thy full heart to God above,
  Seeking in solitudes the gentler light
  Of woods and wilds, peace-loving Eremite !
Good Basil ! thy companion gently prove,
  Shrinking from pastoral cares : and may Heaven's King
His service not reject, nor choice refuse !
  Each for his sphere He mouldeth ; each doth earn
His place from Him ; His Dove hath many hues,
  Some lead His flock, while some His praises sing ;
  Some in His inner Temple incense burn.

## HILARY.

[Bishop of Poitiers, his birthplace. For his zeal against the Arian heresy he was sent into exile by the Emperor Constantius in A.D. 356. During this exile, which lasted three years, he wrote his treatise, " De Trinitate." See last line.]

STAR of the West ! when all the skies grew dark,
   And Arian clouds conceal'd Heaven's genial eye,
Christ sent thee forth to guide His labouring ark,
   From His own peaceful palace ever nigh ;
Still where thy Church her annual pathway steers,
High in the Heavens thy radiant sign appears.[1]

Angel of Poitiers, Aquitanian Saint !
   Exile to thee was drawing nearer home ;
For where Christ is was home to thee ;—the plaint
   Of thy bereaved Church doth thence become
Her gladness, when she welcomes thee return'd,
And hails the light which in thine exile burn'd.

[1] The first term in the year is still known by his name.

## CYRIL OF JERUSALEM.

[Born in Jerusalem about A.D. 315. Having taken Holy Orders, he became noted for his power in catechising and preparing catechumens for Holy Baptism. It was in this office that he delivered the catechetical lectures by which his name is chiefly known. He became Bishop of Jerusalem, 351.]

FROM the Archangel on Heaven's highest stair,
  And Seraphim and Cherubim around,
Unto the lowest child of sin and care,—
  To each and all, as meet recipients found,
By Nature's works, or word, or Spirit's seal,
'Tis Christ alone the Father doth reveal.[1]

Cyril, on Salem's apostolic throne,
  Or where the humbler Catechist doth stand,
'Tis Christ in thee that takes each little one
  Into His arms, and leads him by the hand
Into the inner temple, fill'd with light,
And bathes in fountains of the Infinite.

[1] The thought is from St Cyril's Catechesis, vi. p. 48.

## EPIPHANIUS.

[Bishop of Salamis, in Cyprus, for thirty-six years; died in extreme old age, A.D. 403. He was an enthusiastic promoter of monasticism, and a vehement writer against Origenism. His *Anchoratus*, published in 374, was "an Exposition of the True Faith as it had been taught from the beginning," and was so named as indicating that the Faith, anchor-like, saves the mind from being shipwrecked by the stormy waves of Heresy. In his vehemence against the Origenists, the old man, urged by some fanatical monks, actually set sail for Constantinople, and denounced the patriarch St Chrysostom, for his supposed favour to them. He seems to have been pacified, and started on his return, but died on board ship. He is said to have been so generous to the poor that he gave away not only his own substance, but the treasures of his church.]

ALAS ! that strife should come, e'en at the tomb,
    'Twixt thee and Chrysostom,
Good Epiphanius ! by the zeal of truth
    Kindling to second youth.
Though Faith's sure anchor[1] doth thy vessel save
    From error's wind and wave,
Yet 'neath the keel is heard the ocean's roar,
    At anchor, not on shore.
But so the Eremite's stern solitude
    Thy spirit hath imbued,
That heavenly Contemplation is thy cell,
    And Prayer thy citadel ;
And so hath nurs'd to alms and charities,
    That favour'd Salamis
Might deem to thee the gentle soul to pass
    Of her own Barnabas.[2]

---

[1] Alluding to his work, " Ancoratus, seu de Fide."
[2] Acts iv. 36, 37.

## GREGORY NYSSEN.

[Bishop of Nyssa, in Cappadocia, from 372 to 395. In conjunction
with St Gregory Nazianzen he defended the Catholic faith against
Arianism, and probably drew up the Nicene Creed. Being exiled by the
Second Synod of Ancyra by Arian influence, he visited the Holy Land,
but was deeply afflicted to find to what a low state religion and mor-
ality had sunk. He wrote a supplement to his Brother Basil's treatise
on the Creation. See last lines. It is noticeable that he was one of
the smaller number of theologians, of whom, however, there have been
some in all ages, who have expressed the hope of the final salvation of
all men.]

BROTHER of Basil, Nazianzen's friend,
    In love that hath no end,
Brac'd by reproof and knit by charity,
    In holy wisdom free !
Nyssa doth, from her breast by exile torn,
    Her Nicene champion mourn :
But Judah's haunts his reverent zeal hath trod,
    And trac'd the steps of God.
Yet not on Calvary's angel-haunted ground
    His spirit rest hath found,
But that, where'er God is, from earthly woes
    The Pilgrim finds repose.
He gathers up Truth's fragments that remain
    In Basil's golden strain ;
And goes to seek him in his unseen rest,
    Asleep on Jesus' breast.

## CHRYSOSTOM.

[John, called Chrysostom, *i.e.*, "Golden-mouth," on account of his eloquence, was Bishop of Constantinople, 398-404. His zeal for the reformation of the Church, and his uncompromising reproof of the evil doings of the Empress Eudoxia, caused him to be persecuted and driven from his see. He was banished to Cucusus, a wretched village in Armenia, and there devoted himself to ministering to the sick and poor. But the cold climate and many privations brought on ague, and persecution still followed him because he would not call evil good, and he died in exile.]

PREACHER and Saint, whose name is Eloquence,
  Well call'd they "Golden" thine impassion'd tongue,
On which Truth sat, and glowing manly sense,
  And words that stand the fire,—in wisdom strong,

And strong in charity. Th' imperial town
  Throng'd round thee, and drunk in thy stern reproof,
Touch'd by thy saintly spirit; vice hung down
  Her flower-wreath'd head, court-favour stood aloof.

Nor less thy zeal, in Nazianzen's chair,
  That the King's daughter with her priestly choir
Might shine within. While thus thy deeds declare
  Christ's presence, wonder not if fiends conspire

Against thee, forc'd near the rude Caspian main
To drink thy Master's cup, in exile, want, and pain.

## AUGUSTINE.

[Bishop of Hippo, near Carthage, 395-430, the greatest writer of the Christian Church. His youth was one of immorality, and though his mother Monica made continual prayer for him, he seemed far from God, and adopted the heresy of the Manichæans. He has written an autobiography in his wonderful " Confessions." Visiting Italy in his unregenerate state, he was attracted by the fame of St Ambrose's preaching at Milan, went to hear him, was converted and baptised, and his mother's prayers were thus abundantly answered.]

As when the sun hath climb'd a cloudy mass,
    And looks at noon on some cathedral dim,
Each limb, each fold, in the translucent glass,
    Breaks into hues of radiant Seraphim ;

So, sainted Bishop ! in the letter'd store
    Which still enfolds thy spirit fled from sight,
Comment, Prayer, Homily, or learned lore,
    Christ bathes each part with His transforming light

Late ris'n in thee. Thence all is eloquent
    With flowing sweetness ; o'er each rising pause
Thou build'st in untir'd strength : through all is sent
    The Word pleading for His most righteous laws.

For thy sick soul, by baptism's seal reliev'd,
Deep in her brackish founts the healing Cross receiv'd.[1]

[1] Exod. xv. 25.

## CYRIL OF ALEXANDRIA.

[Archbishop of Alexandria, 412-444. His zeal against unbelievers and heretics led him to acts of violence, and to this spirit the poet alludes. His great controversy was with the Nestorians. A striking picture of him will be found in Kingsley's *Hypatia*.]

THE sword which Christ on earth hath sent,
  With olive branches twine :
To suffer it with meek content,
  But not to wield be thine ;
Tho' round thy throne in tumult strong
Thine Alexandrians loudly throng ;
Yet He into thy wounds shall pour His oil and wine.

Be thine the keener edge to wield
  Of the unfailing Word ;
And shelter with the Spirit's shield
  The doctrine of the Lord !
Where Ephesus [1] hath guarded well
  The mother of Emmanuel,
And from Nestorian leav'n the Church again restor'd.

---

[1] The first Council of Ephesus declared, that the Virgin Mary was rightly called the mother of God, which Nestorius had denied.

## JEROME.

[The greatest biblical student and commentator that ever lived, born in Dalmatia about A.D. 345, died at Bethlehem 420. He had taken up his residence at Rome, and was secretary to Pope Damasus, but his "sterner mood" gave offence in the imperial city, and he went to the Holy Land and founded a great monastery at Bethlehem. The Latin version of the Holy Scriptures, called the Vulgate, because made for the use of the common people, was partly made, partly edited by him.]

THE peaceful star of Bethlehem
    Came o'er thy solitude,
The radiance of that heavenly gem
    Lit up thy sterner mood;
Yea, like a star in murky wells,
Cheering the bed where darkness dwells,
The images of earth its happier light imbued.

The thought of the Eternal Child
    Upon thy cloistral cell
Must sure have cast an influence mild,
    And, like a holy spell,
Have peopled that fair Eastern night
With dreams meet for an Eremite,
Beside that cradle poor bidding the world farewell.

𝕿𝖍𝖊 𝕰𝖆𝖘𝖙𝖊𝖗𝖓 𝖂𝖎𝖓𝖉𝖔𝖜.

## THE CRUCIFIXION.

" Seeing we are compassed about with so great a cloud of witnesses,
. . . let us run with patience the race that is set before us,
" Looking unto Jesus, the Author and Finisher of our Faith." HEB.
xii. 1, 2.

If there be aught of health in these Thy Saints,
　　　Reliev'd from mortal taints,
'Tis but that they their feeble thoughts have rais'd,
　　　And upon Thee have gaz'd ;
And follow'd Thee from Bethlehem's lowly room,
　　　To Calvary's solemn gloom.
Then let us hang our eyes and hearts on Thee,
And dwell upon Thy dying agony
　　　On the accursed tree !
There let us flee, as to a holy tower
Against the world ; and learn the silent power
　　　Of that sad awful hour !
Thy suffering opes to us the heavenly gate,
And nought to Thee can raise our fallen state,
　　　But our own selves to hate :
For suffering only and self-sacrifice
Can fix the heart where Faith her God descries—
　　　Within the op'ning skies.
From Bethlehem's stable, with the beasts around,
To Calvary, 'tween two thieves on cursed ground,
　　　Thou didst with griefs abound,
And, like a cloke, wrap round Thee all our shame,
While rough rude words of mockery mar Thy name,
　　　And toil and pain Thy frame.
Tamar and Rahab stain thy lineage ;
Foul Egypt cradles Thy first tender age,
　　　Judah pursues with rage.

Nazareth, of evil name, Thy childhood rears,
And then drives from her; next Thy sojourn bears,
     But nurseth more Thy tears,
Capernaum, worse than Sodom. No kind roof
Shelters Thee ; Thine own household stand aloof,
     Or taunt with cold reproof.
Thy Kingly court a Galilean few,
And scorn'd by Galilean and by Jew,
     An outcast heathen crew.
Thy Kingly Coming to Thy Salem proud,
Was sitting at a leper's 'mid the crowd,
     Anointed for Thy shroud.
Thine entrance, for the King of sorrows meet,
Was shedding tears o'er Thine imperial seat
     Rejoicing at Thy feet.
Not only Thine High-Priest hath witness borne,
But the whole Council, met on that dread morn,—
     And Herod in his scorn,—
And the whole people,—yea, for these sole ends
The Pharisee and Sadducee are friends.
     A chosen one that tends
Thy watchings and Thy walks is found alone
The fit Arch-traitor ; Thine own Twelve disown ;
     E'en Peter hath not known.
They for a murderer cry aloud, nor cease,
Lest a relenting heathen should release,
     And spare the Prince of Peace.
E'en now Thine innocent sides with scourging bleed,
That Pity from their bleeding mouths might plead ;
     But they hear not, nor heed.
The very scorn of men, a trampled worm,
The winds Thou temperest to each tender form,—
     Thyself dost bear the storm !
Now rais'd on high, a Kingly throne is given ;
Thine outstretch'd hands with fangs of iron riven :
     O sight for earth and Heaven !
'Mid dead men's bones and many an uncouth thing,
And such a crown and such apparelling,
     Full meet for such a King !
And we would be Thy subjects ; o'er and o'er
     The world for evermore

Acts the same part against thee, still the same
　　Tho' with a different name—
Caiaphas, Herod, Judas :—John alone
　　Beneath Thy Cross is known.

———————

"I heard a great voice out of Heaven, saying, Behold, the tabernacle of God is with men, and He will dwell with them. . . ."
—Rev. xxi. 3.

## 𝕮𝖍𝖊 𝕯𝖊𝖕𝖆𝖗𝖙𝖚𝖗𝖊.

Such is the vision our forefathers plann'd,
Pillaring strength in stones, and making these
Melodious, joining Nature's choral band ;
The brooks were vocal, calling on the trees ;
The trees made answer with the fitful breeze,
And call'd on birds, and their responsive lays
Call'd upon man : he moulding mighty seas
Of music carried on his Maker's praise,
For Angels to bear on through Heaven's eternal days.

But now, our honour'd Minster, living Rock
Of pinnacles and cornice sculptur'd high,
Loud is the strife of tongues,[1] which seems to mock
Thy venerable shadow standing by,
And stop in thee thy music of the sky !
What though forlorn and old, thou hast a tongue,
Each shrine and tomb within thee seems to cry ;—
What though thy babes [2] be silenc'd and thy song,
Thy stones shall plead aloud, and live to speak the wrong.

Beauty of holiness, still let me hold
Thy mantle skirts, and talk with thee awhile,
And read thy brow, which fairer seems when old ;
Time's fingers rude, which other things defile,
Make thee more lovely ; and we would beguile
Our exile gazing on thee ; come from Heaven
Thou dost to Heaven return ; and thy last smile
Is loveliest, in thy grief to parting given,
As in the distant isle the lingering ray of Even.

Beautiful Vision, let me hold thee still,
And gaze on thee,—smiling thou seem'st to fly,
And flying still to smile.   If 'tis Heaven's will

[1] Debates in Parliament on the Cathedral Act, A.D. 1 40.
[2] St Luke xix. 40.

Thou shouldst depart 'mong things that are gone by,
In thy hands bear me with thee to the sky,
Angelic Vision ! I no more would mourn
The goodliest things that pass from mortal eye,
But hold thee in thy flight, and with thee borne
Mount to the heavenly gate, the threshold of the morn.

# NOTES.

### The Western Front.

It will be observed, that Faith forms the entrance to that aisle which is termed the Creed; Obedience, to Holy Scripture; and Repentance, to the Lord's Prayer.

### The Cloisters.

On passing from the Western Front, on one side are the Cloisters, an inclosed square with openings or windows on each side, looking into the court. Texts (which are here attached to the Sonnets) are sometimes written up in these Cloisters, as, I believe, is the case on the south side of the Cloisters at Canterbury. They are intended as an ambulatory, or place of meditation.

### The Chapter-house.

This is generally of an octagonal shape, whose eight equal sides are here represented in the eight subjects under the head of Episcopacy. It is often supported by a single pillar, springing up in the centre, which might be taken as an emblem of the one Bishop of the Diocese; and if it be allowable to carry on this allusion, the surrounding seats might be considered as indicative of the presence of the Presbytery; as it is here that they meet to elect their Bishop.

I

## The Porches.

There are instances of two Porches, though one only on the south side is more usual. The exact uniformity and correspondence with which the two sides of the Nave have been constructed, including the Oratories, Sepulchral Recesses, &c., (which it may be observed most closely answer to each other even to the structure of the verse,) may appear to be beyond the precision required from the example of any of our Cathedrals. But it has been thought, that the regularity at which Architecture aims might be more conducive to bring before the mind the end proposed by these associations. And there are higher reasons than these ; viz. from the model of the Temple of Jerusalem, and that shadowed forth by the Prophet. Of the former we read, "And he put five bases on the right side of the house, and five on the left side of the house ; " (1 Kings vii. 39 ;) and "the two leaves of the one door were folding, and the two leaves of the other door were folding ; " (Ibid. vi. 34 ;) and of the latter, "the little chambers thereof were three on this side and three on that side ; " (Ezek. xl. 21 ;) "and palm-trees were upon the posts thereof on this side, and on that side ; " (v. 34 ;) "and at the side without, as one goeth up to the entry of the north gate, were two tables ; and at the other side, which was at the porch of the gate, were two tables ; four tables were on this side, and four tables on that side." (v. 40, 41.)

## The Oratories.

These may be supposed to answer to the *"little chambers"* in the Temple, as above alluded to, "built against the wall of the house round about." (1 Kings vi. 5.) Their use in Christian churches, as little cells for meditation, reading, and prayer, has existed from an early period. See Bingham's Antiq., b. viii. c. 5, sect. 8.

## The Transepts.

It is well known that these are intended to represent the transverse part of the Cross. And the Texts here selected have been supposed to contain a very striking prophetical reference to the extension of the hands in the Crucifixion. And indeed the figure of a Temple, as applied to our Lord's Body, derives a kind of sanctity from His own use of the same symbol. The Transept, when considered in this light, may shew some degree of suitableness in the subjects chosen to occupy this place, one of which represents our Lord "*in Prophecy*," the other "*in History*." In each case it may be said of Him, that He is "all the day long stretching forth His hands."

## The Skreen.

The Disciplina Arcani, which is made to stand for the Skreen, is the term used to designate the practice of the early Church, in withdrawing from public view the Sacraments and higher mysteries of our Religion. These were carefully kept from the knowledge of the unconverted, till they were duly prepared for the reception of them. This primitive custom was probably rather derived than invented. But the reasons given for its observance were partly founded on a reverence for the sacred mysteries themselves; partly as considering it conducive to the advantage of those who were thus excluded. See Bingham's Antiq., b. x. c. 5, and Newman's Arians, c. i, sect. 3.

## The Choir.

The Sacramental, or Eucharistic, Hymn, commonly called the Angelical Hymn, or the Great Doxology, has been from an early period used in the Communion Service. See Bingham, xiv. 21. c. 11, sect. 2.

The liberty which has here been taken of introducing Angels, has been partly from the received notion of their being present in Churches. In a Church, says Origen, " there are two assemblies, one of Angels, the other of men." " The gravest of the ancient Fathers," says Hooker, "affirm, that the House of Prayer is a Court beautified with the presence of celestial powers : that there we stand, we pray, we sound forth hymns unto God, having His Angels intermingled as our associates." (Eccl. Pol., b. v. 25.) And partly from this being the Hymn which Angels brought down from Heaven. But chiefly because in these two

Hymns, which are used in the Eucharist, the "Gloria in excelsis" and the "Trisagion," the Church was wont to call upon the heavenly inhabitants to join in giving thanks to God; of which see an interesting account in Bingham, vol. v. b. xv. 10, where, among the passages quoted from the Fathers, are the following. "Heretofore," says St Chrysostom, "this hymn was only sung in Heaven, but after that the Lord vouchsafed to come down upon earth, He brought this melody to us also. Therefore the Bishop, when he stands at this holy table to present our rational Service, and offer the unbloody Sacrifice, does not simply call upon us to join in this glorification, but first naming the Cherubims, and making mention of the Seraphims, he then exhorts us all to send up these tremendous words, and withdrawing our minds from the earth by intimating with what company we make a Choir, he cries out to every man, and says as it were in these words; 'Thou singest with the Seraphims, stand together with the Seraphims, stretch forth thy wings with them, with them fly round the royal throne.'" In another place says the same ancient writer, "The Seraphims above sing the holy Trisagion Hymn: the holy congregation of men on earth send up the same: the general assembly of celestial and earthly creatures join together: there is *one thanksgiving—μία εὐχαριστία,—*one exultation, one choir of men and Angels in one station rejoicing together." We have also intimations of the same practice in our own Service, "Therefore with Angels and Archangels, and with all the company of Heaven, we laud and magnify Thy glorious Name; evermore praising Thee, and saying, Holy, Holy, Holy, Lord God of hosts, heaven and earth are full of Thy glory: Glory be to Thee, O Lord most High. Amen."

TURNBULL AND SPEARS, PRINTERS. EDINBURGH.

3 M.—V. 12/88.

# Theological and Devotional Books

### PUBLISHED BY

# GRIFFITH, FARRAN & CO.,

#### ST. PAUL'S CHURCHYARD, LONDON.

## The Ancient and Modern Library of Theological Literature.

Price **1**s. per volume. *Bound in cloth*, 3 by 5½, uncut edges.
The Volumes already published are—

Vol. 1. The Confessions of S. Augustine.
,, 2. A Kempis' Imitation of Christ.
,, 3. George Herbert's English Poems, &c.
,, 4. Keble's Christian Year.
,, 5. The Five Empires. R. Wilberforce.
,, 6. Andrewes' Sermon on the Incarnation.
,, 7. Bp. Jeremy Taylor's Holy Living.
,, 8. Baxter's Saint's Rest. Vol. I.
,, 9. Baxter's Saint's Rest. Vol. II.
,, 10. Law's Serious Call.
,, 11. Lives of the Popes, to the Accession of Gregory VII. By B. Platina.
,, 12. Giles Fletcher's Victory of Christ.
,, 13. The Orations of S. Athanasius.
,, 14. The First Prayer Book of Edward VI.
,, 15. The Whole Duty of Man.
,, 16. The Second Prayer Book of Edward VI.

The following are in preparation—

The Tutor. By S. Clement of Alexandria, with Life.
The Practice of Piety.
Selections from S. Bernard.
The Shepherd of Hermas and Epistles of SS. Clement, Ignatius and Polycarp.
Select Sermons by S. John Chrysostom.
Sermons by Massillon.

Romain's Walk of Faith.
Bishop Wilberforce's Sermons.
The Apologies of Tertullian and Justin Martyr.
Lives of the Popes, Vol. II. Gregory VII. to Sextus IV.
Lives of the Popes, Vol. III. Reformation Period Reviews, 2nd of Edward VI.

"A marvellously cheap reproduction. This series will render accessible to the many works which have hitherto been beyond the reach of any but the few."--*Church Quarterly Review.*

"The more purchasers and readers the series shall obtain the better for the diffusion of correct notions upon theological subjects."—*Literary Churchman.*

"Capitally printed, we congratulate all parties concerned on the bringing out of this aspirant to the appreciation of the reading public."—*Church Review.*

"The effort has our hearty approval."—*Literary World.*

"Our obligations to the publishers are very great."—*Gospeller.*

"The whole series would be an acquisition to any theological Library."—*Manchester Courier.*

"There is a mine of wealth in these old-time discourses on religious topics."—*Western Daily News.*

# The Altar Hymnal.

With an Introduction by the Rev. Canon CARTER. The Music Edited by Mr. A. H. BROWN. Contains the Introits, Graduals, Alleluias, Tracts, Offertories, and Communions for the whole of the Christian Year, also Processionals, Sequences, and Special Hymns for use at the Offertory and Ablutions on all Greater Days, as well as a large Collection of Eucharistic Hymns, for general use on ordinary occasions.

Musical Edition, cloth, price **5**s.

——————————— Bevelled boards, red edges, price **6**s.

Words only, cloth, flush, price **1**s.; cloth boards, red edges **1**s. **3**d.

APPLICATIONS FOR GRANTS to assist in the introduction of the "Altar Hymnal" into poor churches should be addressed to the " Compilers," care of Mr. W. Plimpton, 39, Lombard Street, London.

"A book of considerable interest and value . . . We cannot close without noting the extraordinary number of good and new hymns here collected."—*Literary Churchman.*
" The doctrinal standard of the book is excellent."—*Northern Churchman.*
" The most satisfactory hymnal that has appeared. We can readily accord the highest commendation."—*John Bull.*
" The introduction of the ' Altar Hymnal' is calculated to do more for the advancement of the people in reverence and knowledge than many sermons."—*Church Times.*

# The Preacher's Promptuary of Anecdote:

Stories New and Old, Arranged, Classified, and Indexed for the use of Preachers, Teachers, and Catechists. By the Rev. W. FRANK SHAW, B.D., Vicar of Eastry, Kent. 100 short and pithy Stories, each pointing some moral or illustrating some doctrine. Crown 8vo, cloth boards, price **2**s. **6**d.

" Its Church tone is irreproachable. . . . . . A rare attribute of books of anecdotes."—*Literary Churchman.*
" The selection is good and varied."—*Literary World.*
" Will be found as suitable for the teacher as for the preacher."—*Schoolmistress.*

# A Manual for Communicants' Classes.

By the same Author.

Short offices for use on ordinary occasions and before the Greater Festivals, together with very full notes of addresses on various aspects of the Holy Eucharist, a special series on its Types, together with a Commentary on the English Communion Office, and other useful matter. Cloth boards, price **3**s. **6**d.

"The substance of the Manual is as good as the order of it."—*Guardian.*
" Bears marks of ability, thoroughness, and scholarship."—*Sunday School Chronicle.*
" The types of the Eucharist are specially well treated. We do not remember so perfect an arrangement for the instruction of classes carried out before."—*Church Times.*
" A store of materials for lectures to communicants."—*Church Bells.*
" Space would fail us to catalogue, much more to describe these excellent chapters Mr. Shaw has supplied a need, and we hope that the volume will meet with all the success it deserves."—*Church Review.*
" We can recommend this book to the clergy."—*Literary Churchman.*

*Office* separately, Paper **3**d., Cloth **6**d.

# A Manual for Confirmation Classes.

By the Author of " A Manual for Communicants' Classes."
Lectures and sets of Questions for use of Catechists and Catechumens,
with an office for use at each Lecture.   Cloth boards, **3**s. **6**d.
" Of extreme use and value to Catechists."—*Bookseller*.
" A useful book, the work of an experienced instructor."—*Sunday School Chronicle.*

The Office and Questions, from the above, for distribution amongst
the Catechumens, may be had separately.   Price **2**d.

# A Manual for the Visitation of the Sick.

By the Rev. R. ADAMS.   Containing, besides the ordinary Services
for the Visitation of the Sick, Special Prayers, Readings, Hymns,
&c., for use either by the visitor or the sick persons themselves.
Roan, limp, price **3**s. **6**d.
" All that a clergyman is likely to need."—*Guardian.*
" An extremely useful Manual."—*Church Bells.*
" An exceedingly valuable compilation."—*Christian World.*

# The Churchman's Altar Manual and Guide to Holy Communion. Together with the Collects,

Epistles, and Gospels, and a selection of appropriate Hymns.
Royal 32mo, with Rubrics and Borders in red, cloth, **2**s.
——————— with Eight Photos, **4**s.
Large Type Edition. cloth, red edges, **2**s.
Cheap Edition, for Distribution, cloth flush, **6**d., or red edges, **9**d.
Also in various leather bindings.

# The Young Communicant's Manual.

Containing Instructions and Preparatory Prayers in accordance with
the Church's directions for Preparations ; Form of Self-Examination ;
the Services for the Holy Communion, with appropriate Devotions,
Intercessions, and Thanksgivings ; Hymns, &c.
18mo, Cloth, red edges, price **1**s.
32mo, Cheap Edition, for Distribution, cloth flush, **6**d.
——————————— Cloth boards, red edges, **9**d.
Also in various leather bindings.

# Approach to the Holy Altar.

By BISHOP KEN.   A New Edition, to which is added the Collects,
Epistles, and Gospels, and a selection of Eucharistic Hymns.
32mo, cloth flush, **6**d.   Cloth, red edges, **9**d.
Also in various leather bindings.

# Bishop Wilson's Lord's Supper.

A short and plain instruction, for the better understanding of the
Lord's Supper ; specially prepared for the benefit of Young Com-
municants, together with the Collects, Epistles, and Gospels.   By
the Right Rev. THOMAS WILSON, D.D., Lord Bishop of Sodor and
Man.   Royal 32mo., with rubrics and borders in red, cloth, price **2**s.
Cheap edition for distribution, cloth flush, **6**d., or red edges, **9**d.
Also in various leather bindings.

# Getting Ready for the Mission.

Suggestions to Clergy who are preparing for a Mission in their Parishes. With a Preface upon carrying on the Work afterwards, &c. By the Rev. W. DONNE, Vicar of Gt. Yarmouth, formerly Rector of Limehouse, E., Curate-in-Charge of Winchester College Mission, All Hallows, East India Docks, E. With a Preface by Rev. Canon MASON, B.D., Vicar of All Hallows, Barking. Revised Edition, Fcap. 8vo, cloth, price 2s.

" Every point and detail in the preparatory work of a Mission is dwelt upon clearly, practically, and briefly."—*Literary Churchman.*

" No clergyman who contemplates a Mission in his Parish should be without this helpful and suggestive Book."—*Church Times.*

" Just the kind of practical help that is wanted."—*John Bull.*

"We heartily commend this book to the consideration of all who are interested in Missions."—*Church Bells.*

# The Durham Mission Hymn Book.

Compiled by NATHANIEL KEYMER, M.A., Rector of Headen, Notts, and Edited, with a Preface, by GEORGE BODY, M.A., Canon Missioner in the Diocese of Durham. Paper covers, price 1½d. each. In numbers, for distribution, price 1d., or in Cloth flush, 3d.

WORDS AND MUSIC, price 1s. 6d., paper ; cloth 2s.

" The best we have met with."—*Church Bells.*

# What is a Mission?

The Object, Preparation, Obstacles, Encouragements, &c., of a Mission. By the Very Rev. REYNOLDS HOLE, Dean of Rochester. Sewed, price 3d. ; cloth, 6d.

# Tracts for the People.

By Dr. R. LINKLATER, Vicar of Stroud Green, N. The series consists of (1) Infant Baptism ; (2) High Celebration ; (3) Confession ; (4) The Holy Eucharist ; to which additions will be made. Price 1d. each.

# Take with you words. A Mission book.

By the Ven. G. R. WYNN, A.M., Archdeacon of Aghadoe. Sewed, price 3d., Cloth, 6d.

# Steps of the Sanctuary.

Being Simple Devotions, together with 'The Prayer Book, and Hymns Ancient and Modern. Arranged by the Rev. ALFRED PAYNE, Vicar of Baldersby. Price 9d.

# A Brief Instruction ;

Or, Catechism on the Church of Christ and Her Ministry, chiefly by way of Questions and Answers. For the use of Members of the Church of England, at, or after the time of Confirmation. Price 2d. Sewed.

# The Christian Year. (KEBLE.)

A Edition, Fcap. 8vo, on toned paper, ornamental capitals, &c.
cloth, bevelled boards, **2**s. **6**d.
With 8 Illustrations by the Collotype process, **3**s. **6**d.

B Edition, 18mo, red border lines, cloth, plain, **1**s. **6**d.
Cloth, bevelled boards, red edges, **2**s.

C Edition, Imperial 32mo, toned paper, ornamental capitals, &c.,
cloth, red edges, **1**s. **6**d.

D Edition, Crown 8vo, Ancient and Modern Library Edition,
cloth, uncut edges, **1**s.

E Edition, Demy 32mo, cheap edition, cloth flush, **6**d.
Cloth boards, red edges, **1**s.

All the above five editions are kept in a variety of leather bindings.

# Of the Imitation of Christ. (À KEMPIS.)

A newly revised translation.

A Edition, Crown 8vo, large type, superfine paper, cloth, bevelled
boards, **2**s. **6**d.
With Illustrations, **3**s. **6**d.

B Edition, 18mo, red border lines, cloth, plain, **1**s. **6**d.
Cloth, bevelled boards, red edges, **2**s.
With Illustrations, **1**s. each extra.

C Edition, 18mo, same as above, without red border lines, cloth,
plain, **1**s.
Cloth, bevelled boards, **1**s. **6**d.
With Illustrations, **1**s. each extra.

D Edition, Crown 8vo, Ancient and Modern Library Edition, cloth,
uncut edges, **1**s.

E Edition, 32mo, cloth flush, **6**d.
Cloth, red edges, **1**s.
With Illustrations, **1**s. each extra.

The above five editions are all kept in a variety of leather bindings.

# The Crown of Life.

A Volume of Verses for the Seasons of the Church. By Mrs.
HERNAMAN. Cloth elegant, price **5**s. Arranged for the Sundays
and Holy-days of the Church's Year.

" Thoroughly Catholic in tone and sentiment."—*Church Times.*
" Worthy of a place in any collection of church psalmody."—*Christian World.*
" Originality and rhythmic power."—*Literary Churchman.*

## BOOKS FOR LENT AND EASTER.

# Simple Thoughts for the Forty Days of Lent.

With an Introduction by the Rev. R. W. RANDALL, of Clifton. Price **3**d. sewed; **6**d. cloth.

" Brief meditations expressed in the plainest language."—*Guardian.*

# A Lent Manual for Busy People.

Adapted also for the Young. Sound Doctrine in Simple Language. Price, sewed, **3**d.; or cloth limp, red edges, **6**d.

" After careful examination, we most cordially recommend it. Its Church tone is most sound and its teaching definite, simple, and practical. It ought to be circulated by thousands."—*John Bull.*

# Helps to a Holy Lent.

By the Right Rev. F. D. HUNTINGTON, Bishop of Central New York. New and Cheaper Edition. Fcap. 8vo., cloth boards, red edges, price **2**s. **6**d.

" One of the most telling and incisive books."—*Church Bells.*

# The Seven Words on the Cross, and other Hymns. By S. M. C. With Two full-page Illustrations.

Printed in red and black upon best hand-made paper, and bound in parchment covers. Royal 16mo, price **3**s. **6**d.

" Really excellent work."—*Church Times.*
" The hymns are admirably suited to their purpose."—*Musical World.*

# The Way of the Cross.

A Metrical Litany for Lent and Passiontide. Words by Mrs. Hernaman. Music by Arthur H. Brown. Words and Music, price **6**d. Ditto, ditto, words only, **1**d.

# Seven Last Words of Love. By the Rev. H. B.

CHAPMAN. Price **1**s. " Brief, eloquent, and reverent."—*Literary World.*

# Holy Week.

A Four-page Leaflet recording the Events of the Passion, Death, and Resurrection of our Saviour. On stiff cardboard. Price, each **1**d. Or, per 100 for distribution, **6**s. **6**d. Postage, **6**d.

# Cycle of Good Friday Hymns.

The Seven Last Words from the Cross. Words by Mrs. HERNAMAN. Music by ARTHUR H. BROWN. Price **6**d. Words only, **1**d.

# The Pattern Life;

Or, Lessons from the Life of Our Lord. By W. CHATTERTON DIX. With Eight Illustrations by P. Priolo. Intended to Instruct and Interest the Children of the Church of England. With suitable Questions at the end of each Chapter, and a Collection of Original Hymns. Cloth, price **5**s.

" This is a very good book indeed, of much sounder tone than most. Valuable aid to catechetical instruction."—*Church Times.*
" An admirable work, well suited for home reading to the little ones."—*Church Review.*
" We commend it to parents and teachers as a very useful book."—*Church Bells.*
" Can be cordially recommended for the thoroughly sound Catholic tone of its doctrine." —*John Bull.*
" Well and carefully arranged, will be found very useful."—*Literary Churchman.*
" A book of which any child should be proud."—*Weekly Churchman.*
" We can recommend it."—*Schoolmaster.*

# Lesson Notes for Sunday School Teachers.

First Series. On the Life of our Blessed Lord. By STAFFORD C. NORTHCOTE. Cloth, price **2**s.

Ditto.    Ditto.    Ditto.  Second Series. On the Church's Year. By same Author. Cloth, price **2**s.

" The helps and hints to teachers are very good."—*Church Bells.*
" Plain, orthodox, and suggestive, and in the highest degree useful."—*Literary Churchman.*
" We ask teachers to get a copy."—*Schoolmaster.*

# The Book of Common Prayer A.D. 1886

Compared with the First Prayer Book of King Edward the Sixth, A.D. 1549. Edited, with Introduction, by W. MILES MYRES, M.A., Vicar of Swanbourne, Bucks., and Rural Dean. With Preface by the Lord Bishop of Oxford. Demy 8vo, cloth boards, bevelled edges, price **10**s. **6**d.

" Invaluable to all loyal Churchmen."—*Record.*

# Historical Sketches of the English Church for the English People.

By the Rev. GEORGE MILLER, Vicar of Radway and Rural Dean. Now publishing in Eighteen Monthly Parts.   Price **2**d. each, Illustrated.

" A valuable means for promoting Church Work."—*Times.*
" Written in a clear and forcible style."—*Weekly Churchman.*
" A very readable and useful work."—*Graphic.*
" A very valuable work."—*Nation.*

# Historical Sketches of the Reformation.

By the Rev. F. G. LEE, D.C.L., Vicar of All Saints', Lambeth.
Demy 8vo, cloth, price **10**s. **6**d.

# An Epitome of Anglican Church History.

Compiled by E. WEBLEY PARRY. Abridged Edition. A short
continuous history of the Anglican Church from the earliest ages,
showing her continuity from Apostolic times to the present, the origin
of her endowments, and her right to them. Crown 8vo., cloth,
price **3**s. **6**d.

"Written in an easy, flowing, and attractive style."—*City Press*.
"We hope the little book will be largely circulated."—*John Bull*.
"To enumerate the good points of this Epitome would require much more space than
we have at command."—*Weekly Churchman*.

# The Book of the Church. From the early British era to

the Revolution.

By ROBERT SOUTHEY, LL.D. A New Edition. 504 pp., Crown
8vo. Price **3**s. **6**d.

# The Church of England. Her Reformation History.

A second series of lectures delivered in the Cathedral Church,
Newcastle-on-Tyne, by Rev. E. B. TROTTER, M.A., Vicar of
Alnwick, and Hon. Canon of Newcastle. Stiff paper, Price **1**s. **6**d.

# Great Social Problems of the Day.

Lessons from the Hebrew Prophets for our time. A Series of Sermons by Rev. E. A. WASHBURN, D.D. With Preface by Rev. W.
Benham, Editor of "Sermons for the Church's Year." Price **2**s. **6**d.

"Well worth study by clergymen who have to deal with educated town congrega-
tions."—*Church Times*.
"Remarkable for the power and energy displayed."—*Rock*.

# Regeneration in Baptism.

By the Rev. G. E. O'BRIEN, M.A., Oxon. Curate of Sacred
Trinity Church, Branford. Cloth, crown 8vo, price **5**s.

"A very vigorous setting forth of the necessity of Holy Baptism and its effects.
Evidently the result of a close study of Holy Scripture."—*The Guardian*.
"We can heartily recommend Mr. O'Brien's work, and trust to find it widely read."—
*The Church Times*.
"An able and scholarly treatise."—*The Rock*.

# Short History of the Episcopal Church in United States.

By the Rev. W. BENHAM, B.D., F.S.A. With a Portrait of BISHOP SEABURY (the first American Bishop), engraved from the Portrait in the Vestry of St. Andrew's Church, Aberdeen. Cloth, price 2s. 6d.

# Sermons for the Church's Year.

Original and Selected. Edited by the Rev. W. BENHAM, B.D. 64 pp. demy 8vo. 13 Parts. 1s. each ; or in 2 vols., cloth, 6s. each.

# Sermons Principally Preached in Haileybury College Chapel.

By the Rev. F. BUTLER, M.A., formerly Scholar of Merton College, Oxon, and late Assistant-Master at Haileybury. Published by request. Price 6s. net.

# The Last Days of Our Lord's Ministry.

A Course of Lectures delivered in Holy Trinity Church, Coventry, by the Rev. WALTER FARQUHAR HOOK, M.A., D.D., Dean of Chichester. A New Edition, with a Preface by the Rev. W. R. W. STEPHENS, his Son-in-law, Rector of Woolbeding, Sussex. Cloth, 5s.

" Of great interest."—*Church Bells.*
" Full of sober teaching."—*Literary Churchman.*
"We commend this volume."—*Church Times.*
" Deeply interesting."—*Christian World.*
"Vigour of style, with a deep and touching tone of devotion."—*School Board Chronicle.*

# Mamma's Bible Stories. First Series.

For Her Little Boys and Girls. In simple language. With Twelve Engravings. Cloth, price 2s.

# Mamma's Bible Stories. Second Series.

Uniform with the first series. Cloth, price 2s.

# Mamma's Bible Stories. Third Series.

By the Daughter of Mrs. Daniel Wilson (author of the First and Second Series), and uniform with the same. Illustrated by Stanley Berkeley. Cloth, price 2s. The Three Volumes in case, price 6s.

" A favourite with every Christian mother."—*North Devon Guardian.*
" We cordially recommend this beautiful little book."—*Schoolmaster.*
" Really within the comprehension of children."—*Daily Chronicle.*
" The illustrations are excellent, the style winning and motherly."—*Western Morning News.*
" An admirable little book."—*Literary Churchman.*
" The language is simple, the type excellent, the wood-cuts spirited."—*Church Times.*
" Very good, large print, short easy words."—*Saturday Review.*
" We welcome this useful little book."—*English Churchman.*

# Short and Simple Prayers for Children.

By the Author of "Mamma's Bible Stories." Cloth, price **1**s.

# Sermons for Children.

By A. DECOPPET, Pastor of the Reformed Church in Paris. Translated from the French by MARIE TAYLOR. With an introduction by MRS. HENRY REEVE. Cloth, Price **3**s. **6**d.

# Christmas Carols.

Specially intended for Children in Church, at Home and in School. The Words by Mrs. HERNAMAN. The Music by ALFRED REDHEAD, Composer of "The Story of the Cross," &c. Price **1**½d. each. Or, complete two vols., paper covers, **1**s. **6**d. each.

\*\*\* The Words only, **1**d.

1. Jesus in the Manger.
2. The Birthday of Birthdays.
3. The Welcome Home.
4. Carols to Jesus Sleeping.
5. The Lambs in the Field.
6. Carol for the Children of Jesus.
7. Christmas Song.
8. Round about the Christmas Tree.
9. Old Father Christmas.
10. We'll Gather Round the Fire.
11. Carol We High.
12. The Prince of Peace.
13. Carol for Christmas Eve.
14. The Babe of Bethlehem
15. The King in the Stable.
16. The Infant Jesus.
17. The Holy Innocents.
18. Epiphany.
19. A Merry Christmas.
20. The Christmas Party.
21. Light and Love.
22. The Christmas Stocking.

The whole Series of Twenty-two Carols with music can be had in One Vol., cloth, price **3**s. **6**d.

"Simple and pretty."—*Literary World.*
"There are few better productions."—*Church Times.*
"Deserves recommendation."—*National Times.*
"Without exception, extremely pretty."—*Christian World.*
"The melodies are good in every case."—*Sunday School Chronicle.*
"Melodies are pretty, easy, and effective."—*Christian World.*
"Words and music are alike admirable."—*Whitehall Review.*
"Highly acceptable."—*Publishers' Circular.*
"Seem in every way acceptable."—*Bookseller.*
"Have only to be known to be duly appreciated."—*Schoolmistress.*
"When known will command a large sale."—*Musical Entertainer.*

# Private Prayers for Morning, Evening, Holy Communion, and

Special Occasions.

32mo, sewed, price **1**d. ; or **6**s. **6**d. per 100, post free for **7**s. Cloth, red edges, price **3**d.

# A Catechism of Church Doctrine.

For Young Children.  By Rev. T. G. HALL, M.A.
Imp. 32mo, paper, price 1d.  Cloth, price 3d.

# Straight Tips for the Race of Life.

By the Rev. G. WHIT-WHITE.  Fcap. 8vo, cloth, price 2s.

"Thoroughly sound and wholesome."—*England.*
" Very useful and practical advice."—*Bookseller.*
" An honest, frank, open-hearted little book."—*Nonconformist.*
" A capital book."—*Literary Churchman.*
" Contains some good hints."—*English Churchman.*

# Devotional Books.  By the Author of "Looking unto Jesus."

Cloth, red edges, 1s. each.
Or French Morocco, limp, 2s. each.

The Eleven Volumes in cloth box for 11s.

The following are the Titles of the Books in the Series :—

| | |
|---|---|
| Looking unto Jesus. | The Footsteps of Jesus. |
| The Christian's Pathway. | Light in the Cloud. |
| The Promised Land. | The Faithful Witness. |
| The Bow of Promise. | Christ in the Covenant. |
| Aspirations. | The Precepts of Jesus. |
| Aids to the Divine Life. | |

" Precious little books, rich in spiritual teaching."—*Christian Age.*
" Present strong claims to popularity."—*Publisher's Circular.*
" Worthy of considerable praise."—*Literary World.*
" Will be of great service to Sunday-school Teachers."—*Christian World.*
" The contents will be helpful."—*Literary Churchman.*
" Will be found useful for devotional use."—*Church Bells.*

By the Very Rev. E. H. PLUMPTRE, D.D., Dean of Wells.

# Things New and Old.

Crown 8vo, cloth, bevelled boards, price 6s.

# Lazarus, and other Poems.

Fourth Edition, with Notes.  Cr. 8vo, cloth, bevelled boards, 6s.

# Master and Scholar, &c., &c.

Second Edition, with Notes.  Cr. 8vo, cloth, bevelled boards, 6s.

# Christ and Christendom.

Being the Boyle Lectures for 1866. Demy 8vo, cloth boards, 7s. 6d.

# Biblical Studies.

Crown 8vo, cloth boards, 5s.

# Theology and Life.

Sermons, chiefly on Special Occasions. Fcap. 8vo.,cl boards, 8s. 6d.

# Christian Believing and Living.

By the Right Rev. F. D. HUNTINGTON, Bishop of Central New York. Sermons. Fifth Edition. 12mo, cloth, **3**s. **6**d.

# Sermons for the People.

By the same Author. Crown, 8vo, cloth, price **3**s. **6**d.

# The Double Witness of the Church.

By the Right Rev. WILLIAM INGRAHAM KIP, D.D., LL.D., Bishop of California. 23rd Edition, Revised by the Author. Crown 8vo, cloth, price **3**s. **6**d.

# The Influence of Jesus:

Being the Bohlen Lecture for 1879. By the Rev. PHILLIPS BROOKS, D.D., Rector of Trinity Church, Boston. Eighth Thousand. Crown 8vo, cloth, price **2**s. **6**d.

# Lectures on Preaching.

By the Rev. PHILLIPS BROOKS, D.D., Rector of Trinity Church, Boston. Delivered before the Divinity School of Yale College in Jan. and Feb., 1877. The Original and only authorized Edition. Price **2**s. **6**d.

"The best book on preaching we know of."—*Guardian*.
"Penetrating and edifying."—*Church Times*.
· "A practically helpful book."—*Bookseller*.

# Mosaics;

Or, the Harmony of Collect, Epistle, and Gospel for the Sundays of the Christian Year. By the Right Rev. WM. CROSWELL DOANE, D.D., Bishop of Albany. Crown 8vo, cloth, price **6**s.

# The Church in the Nation

Pure and Apostolical, God's Authorized Representative. By the Rev. HENRY C. LAY, D.D., LL.D., Bishop of Easton, U.S.A. With Introduction by the Very Rev. Dean Hole. Price **3**s. **6**d.

# The Story of the Cross.

WORDS ONLY. The four following sizes are now ready:—

No. 1. Diamond 48mo....     ... **1**s. **0**d. per 100.
No. 2. Nonpareil 32mo.     ... **1**s. **2**d. per 100.
No. 3. Long Primer 24mo.     ... **1**s. **4**d. per 100.
No. 4 Minion 32mo. red lines ... **1**s. **6**d. per 100.

# ILLUSTRATED BOOKS.

## Keble's Evening Hymn.

With Illustrations from the Old Masters, in small quarto, sumptuously printed on toned paper. Cloth elegant, bevelled boards, price **2**s. **6**d.; or fringe and tassel binding, price **6**s.

## Hark! the Herald Angels Sing.

By the Rev. CHARLES WESLEY, M.A., with Illustrations from the Old Masters, cloth elegant, gilt edges, **2**s. **6**d.

## In the Sweet By-and-By.

By S. FILLMORE BENNETT. Illustrated, cloth elegant, price **2**s. **6**d.

## Annie and Willie's Prayer.

By SOPHIA P. SNOW. Illustrated, cloth elegant, price **2**s. **6**d.

## O Little Town of Bethlehem.

By the Rev. PHILLIPS BROOKS, D.D. Illustrated in Monotint by A. Wilde Parsons and Lizzie Mack. In illustrated cover, Imperial 16mo, gilt edges. Price **2**s.

## The Lily and the Cross.

By E. NESBIT, with Monotint Illustrations. In illustrated cover, Imperial 16mo, Silver edges, price **2**s.

## The Star of Bethlehem.

By E. NESBIT. Beautifully Illustrated in Monotints. Gilt edges, round corners. Illustrated Cover. Price **1**s.

## Illustrated Miniature Text Books.

Containing seventy-two pages, with Text, Verse, and Floral Designs, printed in Colours. **1**s. each.

Faith.
Hope. } Scripture Texts and Sacred Songs. With
Charity. } Prefaces by Miss C. M. YONGE.
Mercy and Peace. }

The Golden Text-Book. Scripture Texts and Selections from " The Christian Year."

"Faith," "Hope," and "Charity" may also be had, Three Vols., in handsome thumb case, with design, price **3**s. **6**d. ; or white cloth, in ditto, price **4**s. **6**d.

## Flowers of Grace.

A Scripture Text-Book, printed in colours. Cloth, price **6**d.

## Our Father's Gifts.

In 4 Parts. Paper covers, price **4**d. each. For Sunday-school distribution. At reduced price per 100.

# TEXT BOOKS.

## The Churchman's Daily Remembrancer,

With Poetical Selections for the Christian Year, with the Kalendar and Table of Lessons of the English Church, for the use of both Clergy and Laity. Cloth, red edges, **2**s.; or with 12 Photographs, **4**s.
Also in leather bindings.

## Daily Thoughts of Comfort for the Year.

By ELLEN GUBBINS.

A book to be much recommended for those wishing for a few words of daily comfort, when longer reading would be impossible. 16mo, cloth, printed in red and black, price **2**s.

## Lift up your Hearts;

or, Helpful Thoughts for Overcoming the World. Compiled and Arranged by ROSE PORTER. The First Part contains Morning Blessings, Mid-day Strength and Eventide Benediction. The Second Part has Thoughts for the Glad, Cheer for the Sorrowful, Counsel for the Tempted, and Victory. Square 16mo, cloth, price **1**s.

## Through the Darkness.

By MARY H. SEYMOUR.

A choice collection of religious poetry, very Catholic in its tone. Cloth boards, red edges, price **1**s.

## The Children's Daily Help for the Christian Year.

Taken from the Psalms and Lessons. Cloth boards, gilt edges, price **1**s. **6**d.

## Anniversary Text-Book:

A Birthday Book of Scripture Verse and Sacred Song for Every Day in the Year. Cloth, plain, **1**s. Cloth, bevelled boards, gilt edges, **1**s. **6**d.

## Bogatzky's Golden Treasury

For the Children of God. 32mo, with violet border lines, cloth, price **1**s. Bevelled boards, gilt edges, **1**s. **6**d.

---

## MINIATURE TEXT BOOKS FOR ALL SEASONS.
### CLOTH, RED EDGES, SIXPENCE EACH.

Gems Worth Setting. By Mrs. GUBBINS.
A Walk through God's Acre. By the same Author.
Cut Diamonds. By the same Author.
Traveller's Joy by the Wayside of Life. By the same Author.
Thoughts and Verses. By ANNIE CAZENOVE.
Whispers of Love and Wisdom. By same Author.
Fragments in Prose and Verse. By same Author.
Life, Light, and Love. By S. W.
Fisherman's Text Book. By S. M. C.
Threads of Gold. By CATHERINE J. MARTYR.
The Churchman's Text-Book for Every Day in the Christian Year.
Watchwords for the Barrack-Room and Camp-Fire. By MISS COCHRANE.

---

## Simple Thoughts for Advent.

With an Introduction by the Rev. R. W. RANDALL, M.A., Vicar of All Saints' Clifton.

Supplies one governing thought which may give colour to each day of Advent, so as to help those who have no leisure or power for very long meditations or prayers.

Price, sewed, **3**d.; cloth limp, red edges, **6**d.

"Just the book for busy, hard-worked folks, and we heartily recommend it."—*Church Bells.*

PRAYER BOOKS, HYMN BOOKS, BIBLES, CHURCH SERVICES ALTAR MANUALS, IN EVERY DESCRIPTION OF LEATHER BINDING.

# PERIODICALS.

## The Rochester Diocesan Chronicle.

Issued with the authority of the Lord Bishop of the Diocese, under the Editorship of A. DAY, Esq., Legal Secretary to the Lord Bishop of the Diocese.

Published on the first day of the month. Price **2**d. Yearly Subscription, post free, **2**s. **6**d.

## The London Diocesan Magazine.

Edited by G. A. SPOTTISWOODE. Presents a complete record of the Church Work of the Diocese. Price **2**d. Yearly subscription, post free, **2**s. **6**d.

"The BEAU-IDEAL of what a diocesan paper should be."—*Church Review*.

## The London Diocese Book for the Year

is greatly enlarged and improved. Full of information most useful to Churchmen, and indispensable to the Clergy, Churchwardens, Sidesmen, and Churchworkers. Stiff boards, half-bound, price (as before), **1**s. **6**d. nett, postage **4**½d.

" A thoroughly useful book of reference."—*Home News*.
" THE book for information about this great See."—*Literary Churchman*.
" Admirably arranged for purposes of reference."—*Bookseller*.
" Well arranged and convenient for references."—*Morning Post*.

## Altar Services.

Containing the Complete Altar Services of the Church, beautifully printed in Red and Black at the Chiswick Press, enriched with Ornamental Capitals, &c., in Three Volumes; one Volume, folio size, 15 by 10 by 1½ inches ; and two Volumes 4to. containing the Epistles and Gospels separately, each 12 by 9 by ¾ inches.

The Set in red cloth elegant £**1 10**s.
——————— Turkey morocco, plain £**7 7**s.
——————— Best Levant morocco, inlaid cross £**10 10**s.
The Folio Volume, which contains all the Services of the Altar, may be had separately—
Red cloth elegant **12**s. **6**d.
Turkey morocco, plain £**3 3**s.
Best Levant morocco, inlaid cloth £**4 4**s.
A few Copies in parchment, Three Vols., £**2 2**s.
\*\*\* The Work can also be bound specially to order in cheaper or more expensive styles.

GRIFFITH, FARRAN, OKEDEN & WELSH,
ST. PAUL'S CHURCHYARD, LONDON.